THE CULTURE TRANSPLANT

THE

CULTURE

TRANSPLANT

HOW MIGRANTS
MAKE THE ECONOMIES

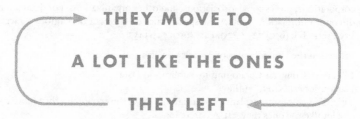

THEY MOVE TO
A LOT LIKE THE ONES
THEY LEFT

GARETT JONES

STANFORD BUSINESS BOOKS

AN IMPRINT OF STANFORD UNIVERSITY PRESS · STANFORD, CALIFORNIA

Stanford University Press
Stanford, California

Special discounts for bulk quantities of Stanford Business Books are available to corporations, professional associations, and other organizations. For details and discount information, contact the special sales department of Stanford University Press. Tel: (650) 725-0820, Fax: (650) 725-3457

Printed in the United States of America on acid-free, archival-quality paper

Library of Congress Cataloging-in-Publication Data
Names: Jones, Garett, author.
Title: The culture transplant : how migrants make the economies they move to a lot like the ones they left / Garett Jones.
Description: Stanford, California : Stanford Business Books, an imprint of Stanford University Press, 2022. | Includes bibliographical references and index.
Identifiers: LCCN 2022022174 (print) | LCCN 2022022175 (ebook) | ISBN 9781503632943 (cloth) | ISBN 9781503633643 (epub)
Subjects: LCSH: Emigration and immigration—Economic aspects. | Culture—Economic aspects. | Immigrants—Cultural assimilation.
Classification: LCC JV6217 .J66 2022 (print) | LCC JV6217 (ebook) | DDC 304.8—dc23/eng/20220729
LC record available at https://lccn.loc.gov/2022022174
LC ebook record available at https://lccn.loc.gov/2022022175

Cover design: Michel Vrana
Typeset by Elliott Beard in ITC Galliard Pro 11/15

Plus ça change, plus c'est la même chose.

The more things change, the more they stay the same.

—JEAN-BAPTISTE ALPHONSE KARR,
1849, in "The Wasps"

CONTENTS

The Best Immigration Policy

CONSIDER THREE COUNTRIES, each economically mediocre:

Egypt

Paraguay

Indonesia

In all three, the average person's income is about one-fifth the average American's, which puts them right in the middle of the planet's income distribution. And these low incomes really matter: about 20 million Indonesians lack even basic toilets, only a quarter of rural Paraguayans have running water at home, and the average Egyptian uses only about one-eighth the electricity of the average American.

So, if you wanted to come up with an immigration policy to make the average person in these three countries better off, what would it be? And better off not just in the short run but in the long run, for generations?

How about this: Let in a lot of people from China every year—maybe 2 percent of each nation's population—for about a dozen years. That would mean letting in around

2 million a year for Egypt,

150,000 a year for Paraguay, and

5 million a year for Indonesia.

Let in anyone from China who passes a basic background check—no criminal record, high school graduate, maybe a little college or some trade school experience—and encourage them to settle down permanently.

Why? Just look around. For centuries, in every country that's had a lot of immigration from China, things go pretty well in the Chinese immigrant community. Lots of emphasis on education and entrepreneurship, high savings rates—not a lot to complain about and lots to like. And when you look at countries where the descendants of Chinese immigrants are the majority of the population—think about Singapore and Taiwan—those nations are models of good competent government, low corruption, and excellent success in the battle against COVID-19. They're comparatively rich, too: the average person in Singapore, for example, is far richer than the average American.

Chinese immigration has a great track record, and here's the thing: China itself is today *just* poor enough, and probably will be poor enough for another couple of decades, that tens of millions of Chinese citizens would welcome the chance to settle down overseas if they had a promising opportunity. So, try this policy: Let almost anyone from China move to any of those three countries, and if they stay for five years, then their next five years are tax-free. That'd spur a lot of people to settle down.

Give it enough time, encourage those Chinese immigrants to raise families there, let them pass on their culture to their children. Then let those children try to run for political office or take on top jobs in the business world. That second generation, as well as the third and fourth, will tend to shape the nation's culture, tend to improve the nation's government, and tend to import the historic patterns of Chinese success that help make a nation's industries globally great rather than globally so-so. Yes, there will be social conflict, there will be ethnic backlash, and there may be racial violence—but while there are no guarantees in government policy, a policy to let in people from China has a strong track record, one of the best.

And while a pro-Chinese immigration policy won't make these three countries as rich as Singapore in fifty years, still, such a policy would be a big improvement over the status quo.

Why? Because immigration, to a large degree, creates a culture transplant, making the places that migrants go a lot like the places they left. And for good and for ill, those culture transplants shape a nation's future prosperity.

THE CULTURE TRANSPLANT

How Economists Learned the Power of Culture

ONE SIGN ECONOMICS IS A SCIENCE is that it teaches you things that you don't want to believe. And this book tells a true story that this economist sincerely, truly does not want to believe.

It begins in the 1990s, when desktop computers grew powerful. In the field of economics, this new supply of computer power created new demands: demand for easy-to-use number crunching software and demand for data on the global economy. Soon enough those demands were met, and economists were combining computers, software, and datasets to supply a torrent of fact-driven research. One big result: a lot more "inquiry into the nature and causes of the wealth of nations." That's the title of Adam Smith's 1776 book that invented my field.[1] But even though you might think economists would naturally put most of their effort into explaining why some nations were so much richer than others, for a long time that question had been a side issue, a scholarly backwater. There were some influential explanations lying around—maybe it's national savings rates! maybe it's how market-friendly, how laissez-faire your government is!—but without good statistics, it was hard to sort out great explanations from also-rans.

But in the 1990s, we finally got the data. So, economists spent the early 1990s running endless statistical tests and publishing hundreds of papers to find out exactly what could predict prosperity and what couldn't. First the easy tests: Was a higher savings rate good news? Yes. Was more capitalism good news? Yes. And so on. Some winners (avoiding war), some losers (inflation doesn't seem to matter much either way—high inflation is more a *symptom* of a bad economy than a problem itself).

The search for the root causes of prosperity continued, and so the search for statistical horse races continued. Every time an economist dug up a new dataset with information from dozens of countries on, say, the fraction of the population that was Protestant or how many coups had occurred between 1960 and 1990 or how far the country was from the equator, it was time to publish a new paper. The research kept on coming—and quickly economists moved beyond looking at conventional economic predictors like

> degree of free international trade,
> exchange rate manipulation, and
> level of education

to looking at geographic predictors of prosperity like

> total size of the country,
> fraction of the country near a coastline, and
> prevalence of malaria

and ultimately to historical and cultural predictors like

> fraction of the population that was Jewish, Muslim, or
>   Eastern Orthodox,
> fraction of the population speaking English, and
> whether the country had been a Spanish, British, or French
>   colony.

A lot of papers found a lot of predictors of long-run prosperity, and while the papers didn't often *contradict* each other, still economists wondered whether maybe, intentionally or unintentionally, these papers were reporting only the results that made each author's favorite theories look good. For instance, maybe some economist out there ran dozens of statistical horse races between "fraction Protestant" and other predictors of prosperity, and maybe that economist reported only the results that made the Protestants look good.

I'm not going to say people were hiding the ball—but maybe they were hiding the ball. It's called the file-drawer problem: if you run a statistical analysis and either you don't like the results or you're pretty sure no editor will like the results, you just stick that project in a file drawer and move on to something else.

By the mid-1990s there was a lot of doubt about whether to believe what you were seeing in the journals. The typical paper might report ten to twenty statistical results—regressions, as they're usually known—and call it a day. That's better than just reporting one result, but it's nowhere close to comprehensive. If you really wanted to thoroughly kick the tires, you'd need to run every single potential explanation of national prosperity in a horse race against every single other potential explanation. If you had a list of one hundred potential explanations and wanted to run them all against each other, head-to-head, two at a time, that alone would be $(100 \times 99)/2 = 4{,}950$ statistical tests. Nobody's outlandish enough to try that, are they?

Fortunately, Columbia University's Xavier Sala-i-Martin was. He wanted to run the ultimate horse race between every possible predictor of a nation's long-run economic performance. He found data from dozens of countries on sixty-two different factors that might predict national prosperity; and then he ran 2 million regressions two different ways, which gave him the title of his 1997 paper, which has been mentioned in over three thousand scholarly papers and books: "I Just Ran Four Million Regressions."[2]

My graduate students always chuckle when I tell them the title—they've usually taken a statistics class or two, and they know how cumbersome it can be to correctly run one such analysis. And this professor ran four million of them! Now that's thorough.

So, who won? Skipping some details, here are the top three:

1. Rate of investment in equipment (physical capital: the stuff that fills factories and offices)

2. Number of years the economy has been open to trade (loosely, a measure of freer trade, low taxes on imports)

3. Fraction of the population that is from a Confucian background (predominantly cultures in East and Southeast Asia)

So, in order: one "normal economics" factor, one "political system" factor, and one "cultural" factor. All were positive factors, so more was better.

That paper's results, combined with other papers along the same lines published in the late 1990s, led to a revolution in how economists saw the wealth of nations. Before then, economists had been spending maybe 80 percent of their research effort looking into normal economics factors, at most 15 percent of their effort studying political systems, and almost no effort studying culture. If economists really wanted to explain the wealth of nations and not just play math games with fancy models, it looked like they were going to have to start studying culture.

And this conflict between what economists were studying versus what looked truly important showed up in the rest of Sala-i-Martin's 4 million regressions. Out of the sixty-two possible drivers of growth that Sala-i-Martin looked at, eighteen factors were able to run his mega-gauntlet. How many of the eighteen were cultural? By my count, five: fraction Confucian plus

> fraction Muslim (positive factor),
>
> fraction Buddhist (positive factor),
>
> fraction Protestant (negative factor), and
>
> fraction Catholic (negative factor).

Geography and past politics were also reliable predictors of economic performance. Across thousands of statistical horse races, it turned out that having been a former Spanish colony, or being in sub-Saharan Africa or Latin America predicted weaker economic performance. Being further from the equator reliably predicted more prosperity: as the joke goes, this explains why Santa's Village is the most productive economy in the world. Together, culture, geography, and the distant experience of Spanish colonization added up to half of Sala-i-Martin's winners, but at the time these factors were consuming far, far less than half of the attention of economists.

Since he published his paper, that has changed. Culture, geography, the shadow of the past—economists study all of these with cross-country comparisons, with laboratory experiments, with theory, and with historical research. This book tells part of that story with a particular focus: I'm going to show how the shadow of the past is transmitted through culture to shape the diverse economies we see around the world today. And I'll show how a lot of what people think of as just "the power of geography" isn't that at all—it's really culture in disguise.

How can I be so sure? Because particularly over the last five centuries, since the great age of European exploration and conquest, people have moved. They've moved in their millions from one country to another, sometimes voluntarily, all too often not. And when they moved, they almost never fully assimilated.

1 The Assimilation Myth

When immigrants move to a place with different institutions, overwhelmingly their cultural values change gradually, if ever, but rarely within two generations.

—Alberto Alesina and Paola Giuliano,
Journal of Economic Literature, 2015[1]

IMAGINE IT: ONE OF THE WORLD'S richest nations, a prosperous example of competitive markets, light government regulation, and relatively competent, classical liberal government. Yes, it has its flaws—its deep sins, regions of poverty—but compared to other real-world countries, not nations of fantasy, it is an obvious success. News of the nation's wealth attracts migrants in their millions from far away—and the capitalists of this successful nation welcome the migrants, the inexpensive labor that will grow the economy still faster.

You might imagine that migrants coming from lands of poverty to a land of plenty would go along to get along—that they wouldn't start demanding political and economic changes to reform this bounteous land. If this economy is working well, after all, maybe we newcomers should let the system keep running just as it is. Most places are far worse.

But no. The migrants, or at least a large, politically organized subset of them, bring ideas from their homelands, ideas that weren't selling back there. Socialism, anarchism, strong labor unions, strands of Marxism—they import these ideas and more to their new home, ideas that were barely on the map beforehand. Immigrants import a new economic ideology.

And because this land is a democracy, more or less, the politicians respond to the voters. First in baby steps, but that isn't enough to please the migrant activists and those they have converted to the cause. And as the activists push harder for socialism, the elites start to push back, even trying to draw in the military to stand on the side of tradition. But military leaders are divided—some think that the socialist activists make a lot of good points, or at least they think that the socialist activists might be a movement that they could co-opt for their own purposes.

And the middle classes—the professionals and near-professionals, the white-collar workers—where do they stand in all of this? This is a nation with a sizable middle class, maybe a third of the population by the standards of the day. They had started off as supporters of the traditional market-friendly system. But the socialists promise lots of good-paying government jobs, jobs with stability, and that has a lot of appeal. And the socialists promised a strong social safety net as well—a source of comfort to an ever-anxious middle class afraid that job loss or illness could mean a permanent move to poverty. The middle classes had long supported the Right, but they are being drawn to the Left. They are now the swing vote.

Ultimately, a fusionist leader rises to power—blending the substance of the Left with some of the trappings of the Right. He pushes for high taxes on elites, he increases government regulation over the economy, and he pushes for higher government spending. His wife becomes famous in her own right, creating charitable organizations that are the beginnings of a welfare state. The nation had other leaders before this fusionist leader and will have others after, with their own stories, but from a distance all are pretty much the same as this one: they offer moderate socialism and high spending and get enough support from the middle classes to win a lot of reasonably fair elections. And the nation goes from being one of the richest in the world to being just another country, only a bit richer than Indonesia or Paraguay or Egypt, in the middle of the global pack but never again a standout, never again a model that others strive to emulate, never again a magnet for migrants the world over. When the magic vanished, so did the waves of migration.

This is the story of Argentina.

In 1913, thanks in large part to a vibrant export-oriented cattle industry, Argentina was a rich nation by the standards of the day. Average income per person in Argentina was 15 percent higher than in France and just 10 percent lower than in Germany. By 2016 by the same measure, France was 100 percent richer than Argentina, and Germany 140 percent richer.[2] Argentina is a failed prodigy: great early promise, little accomplishment.

How did this happen? The standard story in economics textbooks is that for some unexplained reason, Argentina's economic institutions got worse: they went from reasonably market friendly and competent to moderately socialist and far less competent, far more corrupt. But why did the institutions get worse?

Instead of looking to economists for the answer, pick up a normal scholarly study of Argentine history. You'll find quotes like this one from the *Penguin History of Latin America*:

> The Argentine trade unions were led by anarchists and syndicalists; many of these were Spanish or Italian immigrants who had brought with them from Europe a belief in direct action and the revolutionary general strike as the instruments with which to overthrow the bourgeois state.[3]

Overthrowing the bourgeois state: that's an approach that didn't lead to economic progress in the twentieth century. And in "Spanish Immigration to Argentina, 1870–1930," we read: "Anarchism, in the less revolutionary form of anarcho-syndicalism, came to Argentina with the immigrants."[4]

David Rock repeats that finding in his widely cited scholarly history *Argentina, 1516–1982* and shows how the anarchists came to change Argentine politics:

> Anarchism in Argentina first appeared in the 1880s among immigrants from Italy and Spain. . . . When labor unrest surfaced, the anarchists renounced their earlier individualism and plunged into organizing trade unions. . . . For several years FORA [a major immigrant-backed anarchist labor federation] had a major role in [Buenos Aires's] political life.[5]

And the anarchists were quite diverse:

> A Frenchman, Eugène Delmas, was the first organizer but soon he was joined by the Spaniards Jose Prat and Julio Camba, who headed the Spanish section of the Anarchist Confederation (there was besides a French and an Italian section).[6]

The wave of immigration to Argentina had large and obvious effects on the politics of the nation. A 1970 book review in the *Hispanic American Historical Review* described the "overwhelming social, economic, and political shock" of the 1890–1914 wave of mass immigration to Argentina—a period that culminated with 30 percent of the Argentine population foreign-born. The reviewer described "the bloodless revolution consequent on immigration."[7] As labor organizer Sarah Fanny Simon put it in the 1940s,

> these new immigrants [to South America] were the prime movers in the anarcho-syndicalist agitations that assumed considerable proportions, especially in Argentina, during the first two decades of the twentieth century.[8]

And in another 1970 article, this in the *Annals of the American Academy of Political and Social Science*, a professor based in Argentina reframes the story. He sees the mass migration to his country as an example of the great success of assimilation, since the new migrants often teamed up with the rest of the Argentine masses and weakened the nation's oligarchs:

Italians and Spaniards were assimilated better than the non-Latins. . . . It was . . . a success unwanted by the creole elite [of Argentina], which wanted cheap and submissive labor without any of the social changes which weakened the oligarchy's [grasp on] political power.[9]

Any way one looks at it, there's a scholarly consensus: this wave of mass immigration changed Argentine political culture persistently, and it pushed Argentine politics in the direction of populism and government-run industry and away from a relatively market-oriented regime. Economists routinely mention the dismal fate of Argentina, which was once so promising but fell so far behind. They typically blame Argentina's decline on a worsening of "institutions." The economic institutions, the rules of the economic game, used to be good in Argentina, and then they got worse. But they don't mention how they got worse. One major reason they got worse is that new people brought new ideas with them—and those ideas changed the government, changed the economy, and shaped Argentina's economic future.

Importing Attitudes

This is just one anecdote—a story about one country, once. Anecdotes are memorable, but we should spend most of our effort checking to see if this is a regular pattern or just a fluke of history. Perhaps, as my George Mason University colleague Bryan Caplan speculates, people have a strong tendency to conform to the norms of the country they move to. This is known as status quo bias, a tendency to not rock the boat, to instead go along with the crowd. As he put it in *Cato Journal*:

If people have a generic tendency to prefer what already exists, admitting them to a more libertarian society effectively makes them more libertarian: "Liberty is what you already have here. Fine, let's stick with that."[10]

Perhaps that's what usually happens today: maybe, in the twenty-first century, migrants and their descendants overwhelmingly assimilate to the political attitudes and cultural norms of their new homelands. We know that British, Spanish, and Portuguese migrants to the Americas and their descendants didn't conform to the Native American status quo back in the sixteenth and seventeenth centuries, but that was a long time ago. Maybe things really have changed.

Fortunately, there's a vast empirical literature checking to see whether modern immigrants to the U.S, Canada, and Western Europe assimilate 100 percent to their new homelands, keep 100 percent of their home country attitudes, or meet somewhere in the middle. And even better, professors around the world have checked to see if second- and even third- or fourth-generation immigrants—the children, grandchildren, and great-grandchildren of immigrants—still carry some or all of their ancestral cultures to their new homes.

We know this happens to some degree when it comes to food. My Jewish grandmother loved to make matzo ball soup, and while family records are spotty, she was no less than a second-generation immigrant herself, with ancestors who came from across Eastern Europe. This pattern of bringing recipes from ancestral homelands happens everywhere, and of course it's wonderful.

Our core questions, however, don't have to do with food; they have to do with personal traits like frugality, trust in strangers, the importance of living near family, and opinions about government regulation. Do immigrants import their attitudes on these issues, and do those attitudes persist to at least a moderate degree, generation after generation? Is full cultural assimilation to the new country just a myth?

In the last dozen or so years, social scientists have discovered a new way to answer these questions, simple and powerful. They draw on already existing global opinion surveys—typically the World Values Survey,[11] but other global surveys as well. The approach is simple: rather than compare, say, Italian Americans to other Americans and see if the two groups are a lot like each other, this new method compares Italian Americans to Italians in Italy; then it compares Swedish Americans to Swedes in Sweden, and so on. Then we can ask a straightforward question: can you predict much of the attitudes of these different "hyphenated Americans" by knowing what's going on back home? Are Swedish Americans a lot like Swedes? Are Italian Americans a lot like Italians?

The reason we can answer these questions is because the General Social Survey[12]—the standard annual survey of U.S. attitudes, which goes back decades and is widely used in scholarly research—doesn't just ask people their opinions about political issues and their astrological sign (though it reports answers on both of those topics). It also asks people where their ancestors came from and roughly how long ago their ancestors came to the U.S. You can imagine that some of those answers are a little unreliable—people have complicated family histories and often can't remember that much. But that makes any relationship they find all the more impressive: if inaccurate, error-ridden estimates of ancestry find a real relationship, then a more accurate measure of where you came from would probably do even better.

Measuring the Migration of Trust

Economists Yann Algan and Pierre Cahuc, both at Paris's famed Sciences Po, wrote a now-classic paper on the topic and published it in 2010 in my field's flagship journal, the *American Economic Review*.[13] They focused on one particular question: Do you think most people can be trusted, or overall do you think you can't be too careful in dealing with others?

This precise question, with only a few minor tweaks, has been asked and answered in dozens of languages and in dozens of countries over the last few decades. It's the standard way of taking the temperature of a nation's trustingness.

For the planet as a whole, the Scandinavian countries—Sweden, Denmark, Norway, Finland—are usually up at the top of the list. In 1997 this fact showed up in a particularly shocking way: a Danish mother visiting New York City went into a restaurant to eat and left the stroller outside—with her baby in the stroller! Someone called the police, naturally. The mother, Anette Sørensen, was arrested and "child welfare authorities briefly took charge of" her fourteen-month-old girl.[14] The mother patiently explained to authorities that in Denmark, it is totally normal to leave a baby outside in a stroller while a parent pops into a store. After all, who would steal a baby?

It's just common sense that you can leave a baby outside while you dine indoors at a restaurant. At least it's common sense in Denmark, a land with incredibly high levels of trust in strangers.

In some countries you really can do what Blanche DuBois said she did in *A Streetcar Named Desire*: you can rely on the kindness of strangers. That's not true everywhere, of course. In the U.S., children are taught that if they're lost, they should find a police officer, firefighter, or if necessary, someone who works in a shop—and then tell that person that they are lost. But in Japan, the standard advice is different: children are taught to walk up to any Japanese person and tell them "I'm lost." Cultures really do differ.

So much of the economy depends on trust—not 100-percent trust, but good-enough trust—that economists have devoted vast theoretical and empirical efforts to show how trust and its more important twin, trustworthiness, shape the wealth of nations. In the relatively high-trust U.S., people buy stock in companies that they can't really control, hoping that the company's managers will deign to share some of the firm's profits with them down the road. And over the long run, that trust has paid off—both for business owners who'd like to raise money and for investors who'd like a handsome long-run return. But in lower-trust Italy, raising money through stock offerings is far rarer for corporations, and instead, family-run corporations are more common. You might think that family-run companies are charming, but they're often a sign that the firm can't convince total strangers to invest in it. Why won't strangers invest? Because the strangers can't be sure they'll get a fair share of the firm's profits . . . so the company has to stay in family hands.

From believing that the CEO will share some of the profits with the investors to believing a political deal between opposing parties will stick, to believing that your workers will clean the restrooms even if you're not there to watch them, good social outcomes rely on trust. That's why the question of trust begins our inquiry into the migration of attitudes.

Let's start off with the second generation and beyond: adults whose parents, grandparents, or great-grandparents were immigrants. Among that large group, Algan and Cahuc found that current trust attitudes back in the ancestral homeland did a very good job predicting trust attitudes of Americans whose ancestors came from those homelands.[15] Forty-six percent of the home-country attitude toward trust survived, when compared against migrants whose ancestors came from other countries. People from high-trust societies pass on about half of their high-trust attitudes to their descendants, and people from low-trust societies pass on about half of their low-trust attitudes. On average, hyphenated-Americans appear to get about half of their attitudes toward trust from the land that comes before the hyphen.

But maybe that 46-percent number comes mostly from second-generation immigrants, those born in America. Maybe if you looked just at the fourth generation, you'd find that the great-grandchildren of immigrants have become indistinguishable from other Americans. Algan and Cahuc check that theory out, looking only at those fourth-generation immigrants, people whose great-great-grandparents were the most recent ancestors to live their full lives overseas. And what did they find? The same 46 percent persistence.

Figure 1.1 gives an overall idea of their finding. On the horizontal axis, you'll see the average trust level back in the country or region of origin, and on the vertical axis, you'll see the average trust level among Americans—second-generation or more—who say their ancestors came from that country or region. Notice the language: "country or region" reflects the way ancestry surveys typically work. The General Social Survey's question is actually "From what countries or part of the world did your ancestors come?" The list of options is incomplete and includes many but not all countries in Europe and Asia. The list also includes entire regions, such as "Africa," and contains residual categories like "Other European." And remember: if these rough, approximate measures of ancestry have a substantial relationship with modern economic outcomes, that's a sign that more accurate survey measures would find an even stronger relationship. The message from these rough ancestry measures is consistent: average trust levels in ancestral homelands explain about half the differences in average trust levels across these different groups of hyphenated Americans.

This same technique—comparing country-of-origin average traits to country-of-destination average traits—has been used dozens of times and for dozens of migrant-receiving countries. It's

FIGURE 1.1. The migration of trust. Average trust levels in the home region predict average trust levels of Americans whose ancestors came from that region.

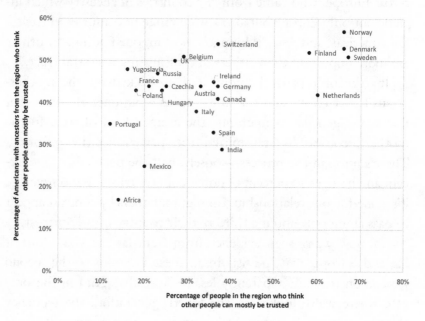

Source: Algan and Cahuc (2010).

rare to get to the fourth generation, but every single study I discuss in this chapter at least reports the attitudes and beliefs of second-generation migrants, people both born and raised in the country their parents had moved to.

You might think that perhaps the U.S. is unique in the way that trust attitudes migrate across borders and generations. But it isn't, not at all. A study of Canadians that looked at second-generation immigrants from various European countries found that about one quarter of country-of-origin trust levels persisted.[16] On average, Swedish-Canadians were the most trusting, and Spanish-Canadians about 20 percent less trusting. A study that compared second-generation migrants to Australia versus to the U.S. reported a big U.S. coefficient—71 percent transmission—and a smaller Australian coefficient—17 percent transmission.[17]

A 2014 paper by Martin Ljunge of Stockholm's Research Institute of Industrial Economics didn't look at just two countries; it looked at second-generation immigrants to twenty-nine countries across Europe, who came from "87 countries of ancestry which include not only Europe but also a wide range of countries in Africa, the Americas, and Asia."[18] Ljunge's most unique finding: "Mothers are more important than fathers in transmitting ancestral trust."

It's the only paper I know of that checked for the mother-versus-father effect, and the difference is a big one. He finds that for second-generation migrants, the average level of trust in the mother's country is transmitted 100 percent to the offspring. There's noise in the process—loosely, half the people get 120 percent and half get 80 percent of home-country trust—but on average it's a one-for-one relationship. Immigrant fathers by contrast appear to pass along only about a third of their country-of-origin trust.

So, now we've seen evidence from Canada, the U.S., Australia, and Europe: trust persists in all these locations to the second generation (though apparently less in Australia). And in the only case where we've looked to the fourth generation, the tendency to trust or distrust persisted there as well—46 percent of it. Since trust is such a critical ingredient in the nation's prosperity recipe, and since this finding has been replicated by so many scholars across so many of the rich countries of Europe and North America, we'll draw special attention to it: on average, about 40 percent of the attitude toward trust from an immigrant's home country is passed on to second-generation immigrants—and about the same 40 percent persists for at least four generations—to the migrant's great-grandchildren.

The Spaghetti Theory of Cultural Change

But isn't cultural change a two-way street? Don't immigrants often change the longtime residents, and don't the longtime residents change the migrants, with both sides meeting somewhere in the middle? And if we take that "40-percent persistent" claim at face value, what's happening to the other 60 percent of cultural attitudes? Do those cultural traits vanish, or instead, do they get synthesized into the culture of the migrant's new homeland, transforming the nation into something new?

Consider the case of spaghetti. The Order of the Sons of Italy—a group I'd love to join if I could make a halfway credible claim to Italian ancestry—says that about 6 percent of Americans have Italian ancestry.[19] Yet *National Geographic* reports that about 12 percent of all restaurants in the U.S.—one in eight—serve Italian food.[20] And everyone knows why so many restaurants serve Italian food: because it's delicious. It's not just Italian Americans eating the pizza and pasta and veal chops; it's pretty much everyone. What started out as a lower-class ethnic cuisine of southern Italians adapted to its new American home—adding more meat, in particular—and became one of the great culinary defaults that's been embraced across American ethnicities.

So, when it comes to spaghetti, Italians came to America, and Italians changed America, making it just a little bit more like Italy. A naïve statistician who analyzed American dining choices might say, "It looks like Italian Americans and all the other Americans are eating pretty much the same food as each other. They're all eating burgers and spaghetti and pizza and hot dogs. It looks like the Italians pretty much fully assimilated!"

But of course, that statistician would be missing a big part of the story: the spaghetti and pizza. When it comes to food, Italian Americans and all the other Americans met in the middle—they changed each other. The Italians took some steps toward the other Americans, and the other Americans took some steps toward the Italians. To some degree, the Italians assimilated the rest of us. It's an obvious point once you think about it, but it's one that too many students of immigration ignore: You can't tell whether migrants are assimilating to the preexisting culture just by looking at the post-migration culture.

Why? Because of spaghetti—because if immigrants change the preexisting culture, then what you might think of as "immigrant assimilation" is each side assimilating the other, at least a little bit.

I call this the Spaghetti Theory of Cultural Change, and it's a big reason why we should spend most of our efforts comparing Italian-Americans to Italians, not to other Americans. In the old days we'd just call it the melting pot theory—a term popularized by a popular 1908 play, *The Melting Pot*, by Israel Zangwill—but Spaghetti Theory captures that meeting in the middle element that's so important for explaining the partial and incomplete assimilation we've seen and will continue to see in the data.

Ethnic cuisines are an obvious illustration of the Spaghetti Theory. A personal example: I grew up in Orange County, California, which became a safe haven for Vietnamese citizens fleeing Communist tyranny, and over the decades, many of Orange County's Vietnamese Americans have created popular restaurants that bring their homeland's cuisine to their fellow Americans. It's now common for our family to head out for banh mi or pho for dinner, something unimaginable in the early 1970s—a sign that immigrants and their descendants are shaping the dining habits of other Americans, assimilating their neighbors just a little bit.

Ultimately, the Spaghetti Theory is just a new way to think about peer effects—about how those around us shape us at least slightly, whether consciously or unconsciously. I see someone mute their smartphone when the curtain rises and the play begins, so I do the same. I see a car's headlights turn on as dusk draws near, so I remember to turn on my own. Our neighbors shape us. In my earlier book *Hive Mind*,[21] I mention other examples of peer effects on human behavior:

> When your neighbor wins the lottery, you're more likely to buy a fancy car that year.

> If you're a checker at the grocery store, and you randomly get stationed next to a really fast checker, you're more likely to start checking groceries faster as well.

> The Asch Effect: If everyone in the room is asked which of three lines is the longest, and most other people erroneously say that the obviously shortest line is in fact the longest, then there's a good chance you'll agree with the mistaken majority. After all, where should you get your opinions: from the wisdom of crowds or from your own lying eyes?

The Spaghetti Theory is built around the idea that we're all imitating each other at least a little bit—and that's true for longtime residents as well as for newcomers. I'd like to see it tested more thoroughly in years to come, but since it's built on a foundation of everyday observation, it's likely to show up far beyond the world of restaurants.

The Persistence of Frugality

In this chapter, we've spent quite some time looking at the long-run persistence of trust partly because so many people have studied the topic of immigrant trust from so many different directions—this is a field where the tires have been kicked for years. It's also important partly because there's already a big scholarly literature across business, economics, and political science arguing that trust (when combined with trustworthiness) is really important for prosperity and productivity. And it's also important because it's just good common sense that more trust is better.

But trust isn't the only thing that matters for prosperity, and fortunately, economists have checked to see whether other migrant traits persist into the second generation and beyond. Two recent papers have looked at whether the children of immigrants to the UK and Germany import much of their attitudes toward saving—toward frugality—from their parents' home countries. A paper coauthored by UCLA's Paola Giuliano, a leader in the field of cultural persistence, looked at whether immigrants from countries with high national savings rates are likely to save a lot of money themselves.[22] She looked at first-, second-, and third-generation immigrants to the UK who responded to a survey asking about financial behavior. The survey asked how much the respondent had saved (in pounds, not as a percent of income); it asked if the respondent had saved money at all in the past year (a simple yes or no question); and it also asked about changes in the person's total savings over the years.

In all three generations, the national savings rate of the immigrant's ancestral home really did predict savings behavior in the UK. But it was especially obvious in the second generation: people whose parents came from countries with higher savings rates tended to save noticeably more than similar people whose parents came from countries with lower savings rates. Whether you looked at the amount a person saved, whether the person saved at all, or how much the person's wealth had increased over the years, the children of migrants made financial choices that looked quite a bit like the financial choices of people in the country where their parents had been born.

It was a hard result to shake. To some extent, frugality appears to be imported. There were interesting outliers, exceptions to the rule: for instance, first-generation immigrants from Ghana came from a low-savings country but on average saved a lot once they got to the UK. But the rule was there: for instance, Chinese immigrants came from a country with a high national savings rate and they had a high level of savings in the UK.

A team of European scholars performed a similar study for Germany, focusing on second-generation immigrants to Germany whose parents had come from a wide range of countries across Europe, Asia, Africa, and the Americas. Cultural transplant theory held true there as well: "Second generation immigrants from countries that value thrift and wealth accumulation more tend to save more in Germany."[23]

They also note that they "confirm [the] results using data from the United Kingdom." Two independent sets of scholars coming to the same conclusion: an immigrant's country of origin really does help predict the frugality of the children of immigrants. Based on what we know so far, it's reasonable to believe that migrants import a substantial portion of their views toward frugality, toward giving thought for the financial morrow, toward whether they act like Aesop's patient ant or like his shortsighted grasshopper. And for a nation as a whole, more frugality means more saving and therefore more investment. It also means a larger stock of funds to push into venture capital, into research and development, and even into college education—all forms of investment, all ways to raise future incomes. Attitudes toward the future are, to a great extent, just a cultural attitude, not a matter of right or wrong. And migrants can, to a great extent, transplant those cultural attitudes from one nation to another.

The Perils of Family Values

Who doesn't love a close-knit family? The grinding hand of capitalism, that's who. If you decide you're going to live close to your mom and dad, come what may, that means that you'll search only for careers close to where they live; it means you can't search far and wide for the best opportunity; and it means you're less likely to find the best possible match for your unique skills. That's one of the key but obvious insights of what economists call the search theory of labor markets: you'll probably find a better job if you can look beyond the town you were born in. A bigger search pool usually means a better match.

Of course, it's good to let people follow their own wishes about how close to stay to their families, but at the same time researchers should find out the social consequences of close-knit families. And here again the migration literature points the way. This time it was four authors, the France-based scholars Algan and Cahuc we've seen before, along with UCLA's Giuliano and the late Harvard economist Alberto Alesina, who together studied the attitudes and life outcomes of second-generation migrants to the United States.[24] They drew on the World Values Survey again, which asks adults a number of family-related questions like these, paraphrasing:

1. Do you live with your parents?

2. How important is it to respect your parents, good or bad, right or wrong?

3. How important is it to make your parents proud?

4. How important is it for parents to sacrifice their happiness for their children's well-being?

5. How important is it to obey one's parents?

6. How important is family in your life?

So, when immigrants come from nations with strong pro-family values, what happens to their adult children? The authors sum it up: "All the different measures of family values have a significant effect on wages."[25] But it might not be what you had expected: "Second generation immigrants coming from familistic countries [i.e., countries with stronger family values] have lower wages as predicted by our model."[26]

Stronger family values predict poorer families. The effect of home-country culture on migrant wages is modest but real. For instance, consider the percentage of families where adult children live with their parents. In Italy, that's 35 percent of families; in Switzerland, just 10 percent. The authors find that Americans whose parents came from countries with that big a gap in family ties have a 5-percent gap in wages on average—and it's the more independent Swiss Americans who are predicted to have the higher wages. Ef-

fects of about that size show up for all six family values measures—
this wasn't just a matter of cherry-picking the one pro-family answer
that got a big result. The authors also note that stronger home-
country family attitudes predict higher unemployment rates and
less job mobility among second-generation immigrants to the U.S.
It's another reminder than when you want to stick close to family,
that means you can't search far and wide for the best job.

These worse job market outcomes aren't just bad news for the
family-oriented migrant. It's bad news for all of us. Wages are a
strong sign of worker productivity, and the economy is a team project, so if workers are stuck in jobs where they aren't producing
much, that usually makes their coworkers less productive and it
makes their boss's capital less profitable. So that lost productivity
hurts us all—even if it makes for warmer family gatherings.

And home-country family attitudes don't just matter personally:
they matter politically as well. Second-generation immigrants to
the U.S. have the right to vote, so what attitudes are they importing into the voting booth? The authors check for that as well. They
check the World Values Survey to see how people back home feel
about three topics:

1. The importance of job security

2. Whether the government should support declining industries

3. Whether the government should regulate wages

Questions 2 and 3 are directly about what the government should
do, but question 1 is more a sign that you might want government
help than a direct demand—and the authors show that indeed,
countries where people think job security is important tend to be
countries where the government makes it hard and costly to fire
workers. And once again, an "economically sizeable" portion of
those attitudes are imported when migrants from those countries
come to the U.S. They pass many of those attitudes on to their
American-born children:

> US [second-generation] immigrants coming from strong family
> ties countries tend to consider job security as a more important

characteristic for a job. They are also more likely to believe that the government should save jobs or directly intervene to regulate wages. The effects are . . . economically sizable.[27]

How big is "economically sizable?" They find that the relationship between strong family values and political attitudes is about half the size of the relationship between education and those same political attitudes. To speak a bit informally, a sizable rise in a typical person's education ("one standard deviation" in statistical language) tends to turn that person against regulation by about 10 percentage points. A similarly big rise in strong family values back in a typical person's ancestral homeland tends to turn that person against regulation by about 5 percentage points. As a general rule, if your nation's immigrants are importing stronger family values into your culture, they—and their descendants—are also importing greater demand for government intervention in the job market.

Attitudes Persist (and Don't)

Let's close with a nearly encyclopedic paper that tested out cultural transplant theory by looking at over a dozen survey questions. A team of scholars at the London School of Economics looked at attitude persistence among immigrants who moved from one European country to another.[28] In the second generation, ancestral-country attitudes on three questions were very persistent, heavily transplanted from the ancestral country to the new home. Paraphrasing, the questions were these:

If people don't work, do they turn lazy?

Who is responsible for taking care of a person: the individual or the state?

Does a preschool child suffer if the mother works outside the home?

On four more questions, ancestral-country attitudes were moderately persistent into the second generation but showed more fade-out than the above three. These cultural transplants were real, but nowhere close to complete. Again paraphrasing:

Do you trust the European Union government?

Do you think most people can be trusted?

How important is family to you?

How important is God to you?

There were quite a few questions where fade-out was essentially complete, where ancestral-country attitudes had no bite at all. These cultural transplants failed almost completely. A few examples:

Is it bad for women to work outside the home?

Can the police be trusted?

Are you religious?

Are immigrants a strain on the welfare system?

So, some attitudes from the ancestral country get transplanted to the second generation, and some don't. But among the attitudes that substantially survive migration, many matter for the wealth of nations: savings rates, views on trust, and views toward government regulation and personal responsibility. I'm glad my grandmother brought her ancestors' matzo ball soup recipe from Eastern Europe; that's a treasure. It's important to remember that people can bring lots of wonderful things from their ancestral homelands—and that some countries are more likely than other countries to export the kinds of attitudes that build a nation's prosperity.

2 Prosperity Migrates

In this paper we pursue the issue of migration's role in shaping the current economic landscape.

—Louis Putterman and David Weil,
Quarterly Journal of Economics, 2010[1]

THERE'S AN OLD SAYING IN PSYCHOLOGY: "The best predictor of future behavior is past behavior." It's one way psychologists remind each other that people don't change that much over time, that improvement is hard, that New Year's resolutions almost always fail. The kids who were near the top of their class in high school usually show up to the twenty-year reunion with better jobs, better lives than most of their classmates.

And that pattern doesn't hold just within a lifetime—it holds between lifetimes. The philosopher and all-around genius Bertrand Russell drew out that lesson when he was asked, toward the end of his ninety-seven years, the secret to living a long life: "Choose your parents wisely."[2] Apples, trees, and all that. Whether you believe the reason is mostly genetics, mostly upbringing, or some mix of the two, the pattern of persistence is still there.

The same general principle—the persistence of outcomes, good or bad, for reasons we may or may not fully understand—seems to

be true for entire peoples, for entire cultures. In the Old World—
Europe, Asia, Africa—the economic rankings haven't changed all
that much since

> *Columbus sailed the ocean blue*
> *Way back in 1492.*

It takes some ingenuity to make competent comparisons across
the centuries, but my fellow economists, with the indispensable assistance of anthropologists, historians, and even geneticists, have
made real progress in measuring the past—and in measuring how
the economic legacies of the past have migrated.

Taking the Measure of the Old World

Consider East Asia's economy just before 1500. In the 1400s, China's Ming dynasty was a powerful government with a large, competent bureaucracy that spanned a region about the size of the modern
U.S., and that government oversaw a population of about 100 million souls. By that measure the Ming dynasty was at least 50 percent
larger than the Roman Empire at its height. Economically, Ming
China was the time when the "sprouts of capitalism" (資本主義萌
芽) are said to have grown, and growing prosperity gave birth to
merchant classes quite independent of the state—in ways, becoming less like tradition-focused medieval Italy and becoming just a
bit more like the business-focused Netherlands of the Renaissance.

Late in the 1400s, Japan plunged into its Warring States period,
but the fine workmanship of the era's katana blades, the elegance of
the temple architecture, and even the size of Kyoto—with around
200,000 residents, as large as Paris at the time—testify to Japan's
robust economic life and to its complex market-oriented economy.
This was an era in Japan's history when prosperous merchants were
referred to as "men of virtue," a sign of a nation that respected
bourgeois success.[3] And in the Korea of the 1400s, King Sejong
the Great didn't just invent the Hangul script, the simple, excellent phonetic alphabet still universally embraced in Korea today.

Sejong also encouraged agricultural science—publishing a book literally entitled *Straight Talk on Farming*—and encouraged the rise of Confucianism (really, neo-Confucianism), a philosophy that, as we've seen in the Introduction, is a strong predictor of national prosperity.

In the 1400s the Italian Renaissance was creating artistic miracles in Rome, Florence, and Venice at which we still marvel, and Dante's *Inferno* was already a century old. In Northern Europe's Low Countries, the economic center of Bruges, the Venice of the North, was in a golden age, and van Eyck's *Arnolfini Portrait* (the one with the bride in green, the groom in dark colors, and the small, curved mirror, where you can see two more people in the reflection) pointed toward the power of science to improve art. Meanwhile, the Islamic world was already well into its period of decline: yes, the Turkish conquest of Constantinople in 1453 was a shock to Europe and looked like it could be a sign of conquests to come, but instead it was the climax—more the anti-climax—of Islamic expansion in Western Eurasia. The great age of Islamic science, mathematics, and technical innovation had ended over a century before, with the Mongol sack of Baghdad in 1258. And at least for scholars living and working in the Islamic world, that wondrous age has yet to return.

And most tragically, Africa south of the Sahara had by far the weakest economies of the three great regions then, a fact that holds today. In 1500, sub-Saharan Africa had fewer people per square mile than Europe or East Asia. That's important because people per square mile is a useful indicator of prosperity in the pre-modern world: population density can tell us a lot about national productivity, since especially in pre-modern times, population density was a sign that farmers could produce a lot of food. That's because more food per farmer meant higher fertility, fewer hunger- and malnutrition-related deaths, longer lives, and hence more people per square mile. By this measure there was more prosperity in West and East Africa just south of the Sahara Desert than in the rest of sub-Saharan Africa—the West African nation of Ghana, for instance, perhaps had half the people per square mile of Greece at the time.[4]

But by any measure, agricultural productivity across sub-Saharan Africa was low. And without widespread long-distance trade, low productivity for farmers surely meant low regional incomes.

Over the next five centuries, people from all these regions moved around the world—some gladly, some reluctantly, and millions only because they were kidnapped and enslaved. How did these migrants—the term I'll use for all these movers, whether their moves were willing or forced—how did these migrants change the new lands they moved to?

The Paper That Started It All

Around fifteen years ago, two economists at Rhode Island's Brown University took up the task of answering this question. David Weil and Louis Putterman ultimately published their findings in 2010 in the Harvard-run *Quarterly Journal of Economics*. The paper has a great title: "Post-1500 Population Flows and the Long-Run Determinants of Economic Growth and Inequality."[5]

By any measure, both scholars are famed economists, and both excel at getting a lot of mileage—a lot of intellectual oomph—out of simple concepts. This paper continues that tradition. They start with a grid—a migration matrix—that keeps track of who has moved where over the last five hundred years. They explain why the question of who moved where is so important for understanding national prosperity: "The further back into the past one looks, the more the economic history of a given *place* tends to diverge from the economic history of the *people* who currently live there."[6] Those words hint at a big idea that Putterman and Weil back up with hard evidence: if you want to understand the prosperity of a particular *place*—a particular country—focusing on the ancient history of the land itself will tell you only so much. A major part of the story, and the more insightful explanation, comes from focusing on the ancestors of the *people* who now live there.

We all know that from the 1500s through the 1700s, a lot of Western Europeans moved to North and South America, and they violently forced millions of Africans to move as well. In addition, many people left China and moved across Southeast Asia, especially in the 1800s as the Qing dynasty weakened and those who were able tried to jump off that sinking ship. Other migrations happened too: Dutch migrants to southern Africa, many French to Polynesia and to the tiny island of Mauritius off the east African coast, Japanese migrants to Brazil, many Portuguese to Indonesia and to the tiny Chinese island of Macau—the list goes on.

Putterman and Weil took great efforts to get the numbers right. For instance, they had to estimate how just how "European" Mexico is today. That meant taking a stand on how to measure multiracial ancestry. As they note:

> People of mixed ancestry are common in many countries . . . for example, people of mixed Amerindian and Spanish ancestry in Mexico. Such individuals are treated as having a certain proportion of their ancestry deriving from each source country. When members of such groups are reported to account for 30% or more of a country's population, we searched the specialized scientific literature on genetic admixture for the best available estimates.[7]

So, while they note that other prominent scholars—including MIT's Daron Acemoglu—had estimated that 15 percent of Mexico's population was of European descent, Putterman and Weil, drawing on genetic studies of Mexican citizens, place that number at 30 percent. And much of that 30 percent consists of people who aren't identified in surveys as "European" or "Spanish"—instead, they are often counted officially as mestizo, of mixed ancestry.

This genetic admixture approach probably sounds less unusual today than it sounded when the paper was first published. Today, many of us are used to the idea of being a one-person genetic ancestry pie chart, made up of slices from lots of regions. For instance, the personal genetics website 23andMe tells me that I'm mostly Irish with some smaller fraction of generic "Western European." That second generic category is 23andMe's way of saying, "We have a general idea—German mostly?—but maybe we'll know more in a few years." Putterman and Weil take that genetic pie chart approach whenever it seems big enough to matter and otherwise use standard survey estimates of ancestry. Consider a few examples of how they look at different countries—and here I'll begin to follow standard usage so that unless I state otherwise, *African* refers solely to individuals with ancestry from sub-Saharan Africa and omits people with North African ancestry. For each country, the set of percentages is the Putterman-Weil breakdown, which uses genetic data when important; following that is an explanation of how the Putterman-Weil estimate compares to self-reported ethnicity:

> *Brazil:* 0.8% Japanese, 74.4% European, 15.7% African, and 9.1% Brazilian. Putterman and Weil report that Brazil's large ethnically mixed population—"pardos" in common local terminology—is half European, and in the Brazilian census about half of Brazilians self-report as "brancos," or white. So, the 74.4% European ancestry is spread around: it is dominant among self-reported brancos and still substantial on average among self-reported pardos.

> *Panama:* 1.5% Chinese, 4% South Asian, 45.2% European, 13% African, and 35.7% Panamanian. Here mestizo, self-identified multiracial individuals are 68% of the population, and just 6% identify ethnically as Amerindian. In Panama, South Asian genetic ancestry shows up particularly in the self-identified West Indian population.

> *United States:* 75.7% European, 4.1% Asian, 6.3% Central and South American, 9.6% African, 3.2% North American. Note that in the U.S., self-reported Hispanics and African Americans alike often have substantial European ancestry: in surveys, 61% of Americans self-report as non-Hispanic White, 16% as Hispanic, and 13% as Black or African American.

This is a reminder: there can be quite a gap between the Putterman-Weil genetic ancestry estimates and our intuitive estimates of ethnicity. And note that from a genetic perspective, Brazil and the U.S. have about equal amounts of European ancestry. With estimates like these for 147 countries along with information on who moved where since 1500, Putterman and Weil had their migration matrix, and were in a position to ask the big question: Is the past prologue?

Which means that they also needed to measure the prologue. They picked two key measures of past social outcomes:

1. How long your ancestors had lived under organized states, or State History

2. How long your ancestors had lived in settled agricultural societies, or Agricultural History

The second, Agricultural History, is easier to measure: it's just a number, measured in thousands of years, and there's little dispute among experts about what that number is. Societies that get most of their food from farmers aren't in the habit of going back to hunting and gathering. And regions with an early transition to agriculture tended to grow in population, in social complexity, and in levels of technological sophistication. It's a reasonable measure of early development—of ancestral behavior.

The first number, State History, a more direct measure of social complexity, is ironically harder to measure, because it's an attempt to capture the *average* history of government in a region between 1 AD and 1500. And over that time, governments have come and gone in many places. Also, some of those governments were run by outsiders, not by the locals, and so those "local" governments are not a clear sign of local skill at running a government. On a 0-to-50 scale, they give a separate score to each currently existing country for every fifty-year period in that territory between 1 AD and 1500. Fifty means you had a real government for half a century, run by locals, that controlled the whole region in that period. If you were a colony for half a century, your score for that half century is 25. If for half a century a formal national government oversaw some parts but other parts only had tribal governance, the scores are lower than 25. And other combinations are possible as well. For example, Italy scored a full 50 for only a third of that 1,500-year period and received a 28 for half of it. That's because much of Italian history since the fall of the Western Roman Empire has been a story of divided rule, with Ostrogoths, Normans, and emirs ruling some parts of Italy while truly local regional governments ruled other parts.

Since so many countries have had off-and-on relationships with formal governance—with some centuries of real statehood and some centuries when village-level or even tribal-level government was the maximum span of government power—Putterman and Weil had to make decisions about how to count past experience. In this paper they "discounted" or "depreciated" past experience, at a rate of 5 percent per half century. That means that a century of statehood in the 1400s counts for about twice as much as a century in the 800s. In other words, they assume that the modern matters more. They then convert all of these State History numbers into a 0-to-1 scale for each country. Some quotes from Putterman and Weil:

> Ethiopia [with uninterrupted state governance] has the maximum value of 1.
>
> China . . . 0.906 (due to periods of political disunity).
>
> Egypt's value is 0.76.
>
> Mexico's [is] 0.533 [recall that Mexico was famously the home of the Aztec empire].
>
> Senegal's [is] 0.398.
>
> Canada, the United States, Australia, and New Guinea [each] have State History values [in 1500] of 0.

The U.S. and Canada, by their estimation, had no organized states of any sort before 1500. If place matters more than the people living in that place, and if State History really is a good index of the ability to take on large-scale, highly productive tasks, then the U.S. and Canada should be poor indeed.

A few Agricultural History estimates, in thousands of years since the end of hunting and gathering, again in Putterman and Weil's words:

The highest value, 10.5, occurs for four Fertile Crescent countries (Israel, Jordan, Lebanon, and Syria), followed closely by . . . China (9), and India (8.5). Near the middle are . . . Ecuador (4), the Côte d'Ivoire (3.5), and Congo (3). At the bottom are countries such as New Zealand (0.8), . . . Australia (0.4), and others in which agriculture arrived for the first time with European colonists.[8]

At this point, we have three big pieces of data:

1. Who moved where since 1500 (the migration matrix).

2. Who began the year 1500 with long experience living under national governments (State History).

3. Who began the year 1500 with long experience living amid settled agriculture (Agricultural History).

It's time to combine 1 with 2 and 3: it's time to see how immigrants imported their State and Agricultural Histories to their new homes. Putterman and Weil call these new national estimates ancestry-adjusted measures of State and Agricultural History, but let's use the clearer term *migration-adjusted*. For most countries, there's been little inbound migration in the last five centuries, so the old news is still the new news—the nations of Europe as well as Japan and China would be good illustrations. But for the countries where migration created big changes in State and Agricultural History, these changes are almost always "ups," since the post-1500 world was, at least until recently, usually a story of immigrants coming from nations with higher scores and moving to—often invading—nations with lower scores. Table 2.1 provides some examples, with approximate values; in each column the first number is migration-unadjusted, and the second number, after the arrow, is migration-adjusted.

In only three nations did post-1500 immigrants push down one score or the other: Kuwait and Israel both saw immigrants slightly reduce their nations' very high Agricultural History scores, as immigrants from India and Europe (respectively) imported somewhat lower levels of ancestral experience with farm life compared to the

TABLE 2.1. **Migrants shaping State and Agricultural History.** In each column, the first number is the migration-unadjusted score and the second is migration-adjusted. Informally, the first is a measure of places, and the second is a measure of peoples.

	State history (0 to 1)	Agricultural history (thousands of years)
Canada	0 → 0.65	1.8 → 6.2
U.S.	0 → 0.56	1.8 → 6.2
Taiwan	0 → 0.90	5.5 → 8.8
Singapore	0.15 → 0.82	4.5 → 8.2

Source: Putterman and Weil (2010).

previous locals. And Botswana's already low State History score of 0.2 fell to a bit below 0.1 as immigrants from South Africa migrated northward in the wake of European immigration to southern Africa.

Overall, though, the history of migration for the last five hundred years has been a story of places like Canada and Singapore, with high history scorers migrating to the nations of lower history scorers.

Testing People against Places

Now, and only now, are we in the position to run our first real statistical horse race: if you're trying to predict modern prosperity in a nation, which matters more: the history score of the *place* or the history score of the *people*? In other words, does the migration-unadjusted or the migration-adjusted history matter more?

And by the way, please don't assume (at least just yet) that this is a story of cause and effect; the scores may turn out to be only signs of some set of traits that helps produce success. For the time being, think of this as the equivalent of using a baseball player's salary this season to predict his batting average next season: that salary does tell us something about the player's overall baseball ability—

it's surely a sign of skill, even if a noisy sign—but the salary itself certainly isn't creating the skill.

As usual among economists, we'll use average income per person as our measure of national prosperity—in this case, income per capita in the year 2000. The results of Putterman and Weil's horse race are extremely clear: for both State History and for Agricultural History, migration-adjusted scores are twice as good as migration-unadjusted scores for predicting a nation's prosperity in 2000. If you're trying to guess how rich a country is today, you'll make a far more accurate guess if you know the history of the people rather than the history of the place.

Consider an extreme case: the United States. Knowing that Native Americans didn't have much ancestral experience with settled agriculture doesn't help you predict American prosperity all that much. But knowing that a massive wave of mostly European migrants came to North America and knowing that their ancestors had thousands of years of experience with farming helps you make a much better prediction of America's modern prosperity.

Let's consider the size, the magnitude, of these relationships—and since we're focusing on patterns, not explanations, I'll stick with the word *relationships* and resist the temptation to call them effects. Consider two nations:

One has a migration-adjusted State History score of zero—so the distant ancestors of the people who live there today never lived under a national government, at least before 1500.

The other nation has a migration-adjusted State History score of 1, the highest possible.

The best guess that Putterman and Weil's simple model would make is that the higher-scoring nation would be seven and a half times richer than the lower-scoring nation. That's roughly the income gap between the modern Philippines and the modern U.S., and only a little larger than the gap between modern China (only a middle-income country) and vastly richer modern Singapore. That's a huge difference based on knowing just one number about the ancestors of a nation's current residents. So even if, by the time you finish this book, you decide that the past isn't *causing* the future, you should still remember that the past does a darn good job *predicting* it.

Turn now to the Agricultural History scores. The range of experience with farming before the year 1500 ranges from a few hundred years at the low end to a little over ten thousand years at the high end. For every thousand years of migration-adjusted history with agriculture, a nation tends to be 31 percent richer. But if we try to guess a nation's modern prosperity using the unadjusted estimates—ignoring who moved where after Columbus set sail— we'd guess that a thousand years of farming experience predicts only 14 percent more prosperity. And because of the miracle of compounding, a nation with two thousand years more ancestral farming experience than its neighbor isn't going to be 31% + 31% = 62% richer but instead will be (1.31 × 1.31) = 1.72 times as rich as its neighbor, or 72% richer. Growth compounds on top of growth. That means that an extra ten thousand years of farming experience predicts 1,370% higher income—more than ten times more prosperity. Ancestral farming experience is a great predictor of modern prosperity, but only when you adjust for migration.

These two extremely simple models have their hits and misses, countries where the prediction is close to the mark and countries where it's far. Overall, the migration-adjusted history scores can explain a little under half the differences in income across countries— that also means that they can't explain a little more than half.[9] Such is the way of the world when trying to use simple stories and simple theories to explain real-world outcomes. If I have a list telling me the heights of a hundred different people and then use that information to try to guess each person's weight, I'll surely do better than if I were just guessing each person's weight at random; likewise, if I know the kind of car a hundred different people own, that helps me predict how much money each person makes, but I'll still usually be off by a lot. Simple models, well chosen, can be powerful by the standards of real-world prediction. These simple early models of Putterman and Weil did all right—and they're just the start.

And by the way, when trying to guess who's the better baseball player, salary alone really can tell us quite a lot. One typical study, from 2003, found that among players earning more than a million dollars a year, knowing just their salaries can let you predict one-fourth of the differences in batting average and half the differences in runs scored across players.[10] Even a crude measure of excellence can go a long way toward predicting real-world outcomes.

Kicking the Migration-Adjusted Tires

Because Putterman and Weil are serious scholars, they don't just report these numbers and leave it at that. They kick the tires on their statistical results; they check out alternative explanations, what we call the "well-what-abouts." One possibility: maybe it's just that Europeans were uniquely brutal in conquering nations and exploiting their resources. So maybe the migration-adjusted effect is instead the effect of the brutal invasion of the New World by Europeans—a story that might then explain the modern success of Canada, the U.S., Australia, and New Zealand, as well as the relative success (at least compared to neighboring countries) of Uruguay, Argentina, and Chile. All are nations that received a large fraction of their current population from Europe, and none of these migrations were close to purely peaceful. Economists often call these countries neo-Europes.

So, Putterman and Weil run another horse race—running the migration-adjusted State and Agricultural History scores for every nation in a prediction race against the migration-adjusted scores of just the countries that lots of Europeans moved to after 1500. What we might call the Unique European Brutality theory would predict that the neo-Europes are the whole statistical story, the main dish, and that for the rest of the world, the migration-adjusted history scores are a mere side dish at best.

But the opposite turns out to be true: The global, overall migration-adjusted scores are the real predictors, the ones with oomph. The neo-Europes are the statistical sideshow, and if anything, the imported history of the neo-Europes matters just a bit less for prosperity than in the average country. So, the often-horrifying migration of Europeans to the rest of the world, while worth studying in its own right, can't explain why these migration-adjusted scores do such a good job predicting modern prosperity. The migrations of Africans and Asians the world over are doing much of the statistical heavy lifting: their migrations matter.

But it turns out if you run a different horse race, it's evident that there indeed is something statistically special about Europeans. The authors throw in a simple measure that's been used before, easily estimated for every nation on earth: fraction of European descent. That's a measure that gives people of European descent the same statistical weight whether they're currently in Europe or (like me) currently in North America. And they throw that into a horse race against migration-adjusted State History. Together, these two simple measures can predict 75 percent of the differences in standards of living across countries, with similar results when State History is swapped out for Agricultural History. Partly this is because there are so many countries in Europe, only perhaps two of which can be considered poor by global standards (Moldova and Ukraine, both of which were poor when Putterman and Weil wrote). Each of Europe's small countries, those with just a few million people—like Denmark or Belgium—counts for just as much as China or India, each of which have over a billion citizens each. But Europe itself has had a good run by global standards, and no other region of the world with that many countries has that much prosperity.

What does this all add up to? First, set aside the horse race, and just consider this fact: If the only thing you knew about each nation on the planet was the fraction of that nation with ancestors of European descent, and you did the best job you could trying to predict average modern income per person using just that one fact, you'd be able to predict two-thirds of all global income differences. Not bad for just one fact per country—and that one fact is doing noticeably more work than either of the other two history measures that Putterman and Weil collected.

But using a modern fact about a country to predict modern prosperity (percent currently of European descent) isn't nearly as impressive as using an ancient fact to predict that same prosperity. After all, if you knew chandeliers per capita or air conditioners per capita in 1980 for every country on earth, you'd also do a good job predicting which countries were rich and which were poor. And in any case, the goal isn't just prediction but understanding—and knowing Europe's had a good run doesn't go far toward telling us *why* they've had that good run. The State History and Agricultural History measures, by drawing our attention to the distant past, tell us a lot more: they serve as signposts toward good explanations of why some nations are so productive and some so unproductive.

What about Geography?

But maybe you're wondering whether these two history measures are just picking up the fact that European and Chinese migrants went to the best places, places that had the geography of prosperity: temperate climates with fewer tropical diseases, close to the water so it was cheaper to ship products. Maybe these history measures are just geography measures. Maybe, for whatever reason, the original inhabitants of North America or Australia weren't making the best use of their fantastic location back in 1500, but ultimately, by the year 2000, pretty much anybody would've done a great job with such great geography. As a story, it sounds like a stretch to me, but sometimes implausible stories turn out to be right.

So, they run another set of horse races between migration-adjusted State History and the following geography measures:

The nation's latitude—its distance from the equator (the Santa's Village effect again)

Whether the nation is landlocked, without access to the ocean

Whether the nation is in Eurasia

How good the nation's land is for agriculture

And as you'd expect, all four of these measures help predict prosperity: landlocked countries have lower incomes; the rest are good for prosperity. But remember, as with the history indices, just because these measures help predict prosperity doesn't mean they cause prosperity. Agricultural suitability, for instance, can't be driving much prosperity in the modern United States, since agriculture overall makes up only about 2 percent of the nation's output. Whatever forecasting power these geography measures have, we should ask ourselves whether it's reasonable to think they're capturing a crucial cause of modern prosperity, particularly in the richest countries.

Let's turn to the results of the horse race: even when the race includes the State History measure and all four geography measures simultaneously—a five-horse race—migration-adjusted State History is still a strong predictor of prosperity. And unsurprisingly, when the horse race swaps out State History for Agricultural History, the result is about the same.

We can sum up the horse race this way: if, hypothetically, there were two nations that had the same latitude, were both close to the ocean, both in Eurasia, and both equally suited to farming, but one nation had a State History score of 0 and the other had a score of 1, a smart guess would be that the higher-scoring nation would be 150 percent richer than the lower-scoring one. Again, this is just a prediction—a story of correlation, not causation, as the saying goes.

But consider this story of cause and effect: what if cultures with a lot of experience living under organized states are a lot more productive because for centuries, people living in those cultures had to cooperate with strangers, work on big projects together, learn to obey the boss pretty reliably, and do all the other things that help make modern people highly productive? It just might turn out that cultures that are highly productive will also be also cultures that are good at taking the best places on the planet, perhaps peacefully, perhaps violently. Excellence at production probably goes hand in hand with excellence at predation. So more-productive cultures will tend to end up in temperate climates with good agricultural prospects and easy water travel, even if (hypothetically) climate, farming, and ports matter only a little for prosperity. People good at being evil will tend to grab the best places.

So, the pattern of facts we see around the world, the pattern that Putterman and Weil report, could be explained in more than one way. Perhaps State History captures just a small part of prosperity, and that one way or another over the last five centuries, cultures with high State History scores got to the big geographic prizes first, and those geographic prizes truly made those cultures massively more productive. So maybe geography truly runs most of the show; maybe location matters enormously.

Alternately, maybe State History is the big mover. Maybe it's a rough measure of some bundle of skills that make some cultures vastly more productive, making it possible for those cultures to grab the best spots in the parking lot of life. Maybe good geography is just the icing on the cake of prosperity. It's obvious enough that those who produce more wind up with the power to get more— and maybe it turns out that one of the things they get is a nice beachfront property.

Why Is Harder than What

This is a problem that crops up any time we're trying to learn about the world but can't run real experiments: Nobel laureate Thomas Sargent calls this the problem of "observational equivalence."[11] Two different theories can explain the same set of facts, the same historical observations, equally well. When that happens—and it happens all the time in economics—the trick is to not give up. The trick is to go out and ask, "What else do these two explanations, these two theories predict? What else can we measure to test out these two theories against each other?" That's the challenge that consumes much of this book—looking for more ways to check and see if ancestral experience is merely a good *predictor* of modern productivity or instead overwhelmingly a *cause* of modern productivity. We've seen that ancestral attitudes toward trust, frugality, and the role of government tend to migrate to new nations and to last substantially for generations, one sign that we're looking at causation. But we'll see more.

The patterns we've seen in this chapter are important, but patterns aren't explanations. Patterns open the door to explanations. In the next chapter, we'll look at other sets of patterns, patterns of persistent technological excellence, which take us closer to explanations. And we'll do something more: we'll calculate each nation's SAT score.

3 Places or Peoples?

Does technology persist within places or within peoples?

—Diego Comin, William Easterly, and Erick Gong,
American Economics Journal: Macroeconomics, 2010[1]

HUMANS ARE THE GREATEST INVENTORS on the planet.

That sentence is true, and it's something to take pride in: people in different times and different places have invented the steel plow, the stirrup, gunpowder, eyeglasses, and the transistor. But only a few of us, a miniscule fraction of all of humanity, have ever invented something worth keeping, worth copying, worth diffusing across millions of square miles, to billions of our fellow humans. For the rest of us—mere consumers rather than the producers of invention—what do inventions mean? We're using them, adapting them a bit, making them work in our particular time and particular place, and sometimes, whether due to conscious decision or unconscious forgetfulness, we're just going without them.

Roman concrete, for instance, the wonder that made the Roman roads possible, has a precise formula that's lost to history. Engineers have tried to replicate the concrete, and maybe they're pretty close to the original formula, but there's no way to be sure.[2] The loss of

Roman concrete is just one example of a much bigger problem: even for great inventions, the diffusion and spreading of great ideas is never guaranteed.

So, great inventions are exceptionally rare, and it's unclear how far they'll diffuse across countries and centuries. But the widespread use of great inventions is both a *cause* of economic prosperity and a *sign* that a society is able to take on big tasks, accomplish great things. Technological sophistication looks like a leading candidate for a third measure, alongside State and Agricultural History, of past economic and social accomplishment.

And unsurprisingly, economists realized this in the early 2000s and created a set of measures of past technological sophistication around the world. They didn't measure inventiveness; instead, they wisely measured widespread use of great inventions. The researchers—Diego Comin of Harvard Business School, Bill Easterly of New York University, and Erick Gong of UC Berkeley—took on the task of creating the three different indices. For each slice of time—which they named 1000 BC, 0 AD, and 1500 AD—they tracked technology levels in five sectors:

Agriculture

Transportation

Military

Industry

Communications

For 1000 BC, an example of communications technology is whether the nation has a written language; it's a simple yes or no answer. By 1500 AD the index is more nuanced: the 0-to-1 score is a mix of whether they use paper, whether they have books, and whether they have some systematic method for printing—like page-sized woodblocks or even better, movable blocks or movable type. There's an enormous amount of historical research into past military technology, so to keep information about the military sector from overwhelming the nation's average technology score, they give each of the five sectors equal weight. So, being tops in communications tech counts for just as much—in the technology index—as being tops in military tech.

And another important note: Comin, Easterly, and Gong don't make the mistake of assuming that, as the saying goes, "absence of evidence is evidence of absence." Before they code a 0 for, say, woodblock printing in 1500, they need to find a scholarly source that specifically says woodblock printing didn't exist in that country around 1500.

Let's take a look at their overall technology scores in 1500 AD, just before migration changed the world. Each number is the average over the whole region, and the score goes from 0 to 1:

Europe (Eastern and Western):	0.86
Asia (East and South):	0.66
Africa (North and sub-Saharan):	0.32
Americas (North and South):	0.14

Africa ranking well above the Americas in 1500 is no mistake, and it's *not* because North Africa is included. Looking only at sub-Saharan Africa, the score is only slightly lower, at 0.30. Around 1500, both Western Africa and Eastern Africa south of the Sahara had well-developed trading networks and traditions of "ceramics, metals, writing, and monumental architecture," all signs of technological sophistication, and well above the overall levels of the Americas.[3]

Comin, Easterly, and Gong point out that although there's a lot of persistence between 1000 BC and 1500 AD—technological rank ordering didn't change all that much over the millennia—the changes among the most advanced civilizations are still big enough to notice. And those "big enough" differences—the difference between winning a global silver medal versus a global gold medal in technology—just might have been the difference between global conqueror and global also-ran. Their four unironically named "advanced civilizations," with their scores across the ages, are shown in table 3.1.

TABLE 3.1. Technology scores of advanced civilizations at three points in time.

	1000 BC	0 AD	1500 AD
Western Europe	0.65	0.96	0.94
China	0.90	1.00	0.88
India	0.67	0.90	0.70
Arab world	0.95	1.00	0.70

Source: Comin, Easterly, and Gong (2010).

So, while China was a touch behind the West in 1500, India and the Arab nations lagged quite a bit more, even though all were still above the global average. And between 1000 BC and 1500 AD, Western Europe and the Arab world had switched places, exchanging silver and gold medals in the technology race.

One way to double-check these estimates is to see if they tell about the same story as an entirely different measure of economic sophistication: the percentage of people who live in cities. There's a long tradition of treating cities as both as sign of technological progress and as a cause of technological progress. The legendary Jane Jacobs made the case for the latter in one of her many great books, *The Economy of Cities*,[4] since she thought cities, even small ones, were natural places to experiment with new ideas, to try ideas out, and then to cash in on those ideas literally or figuratively. The former case—that cities are a sign of prosperity—is the one we all know about: before the modern era, in order to have big cities, you had to have a sophisticated system of farming, one productive enough to feed the surplus food to the city folk. And knowing enough about engineering to supply water throughout a city didn't hurt either, as the Romans knew. Either way, regardless of which is cause and which is effect, cities and technological sophistication tend to go together.

So, does Comin, Easterly, and Gong's tech index predict differences in urbanization across countries? Yes, and in 1000 BC and 0 AD it predicted well over two-thirds of the cross-country differences in urbanization. Countries with a big fraction of the population living in cities were very likely to be countries using a lot of the world's frontier technology. The predictive power of the tech index weakens quite a bit in 1500 AD—explaining only about a third of cross-country differences in urbanization—partly because in that era, Europe wasn't all that urbanized by global standards. Such is the way of simple statistical relationships—a 100-percent fit is never the standard for good science, and there's always a big exception to the rule. But only a fool would ignore the rule—and the general rule has been that urbanization and technological excellence go hand in hand.

So, how does the past predict the world of today? Even without adjusting for post-1500 migration, the level of a nation's tech at year 1500 does an OK job predicting modern income per person, totaling about one-third of cross-country differences. And that happens even though across the Americas, the tech index is trying to predict modern prosperity based solely on the relatively low scores of the pre-Columbian American civilizations. Obviously the index isn't doing a very good job there—or in New Zealand or Australia for that matter—but the fit in the Old World is good enough to boost the 1500 tech index's usefulness for the world as a whole.

But the 0 AD index is useless for predicting modern income, and the 1000 BC index is only slightly better, perhaps solely by accident. Taken together, without adjusting for migration, it's clear that none of these measures can predict half or more of cross-country income differences. Fortunately, it's possible to adjust for migration by using the Putterman-Weil global migration measures—to test whether a history of technology in a *place* mattered more than the history of technology of the *people* currently living in that place. And that's just what Comin, Easterly, and Gong did. They checked to see if with Tech History as with State and Agricultural History, migration-adjusted measures beat out migration-unadjusted measures.

And it's no surprise at all to learn that the migration-adjusted measures are the clear winners. As Comin, Easterly, and Gong put it:

The results of the people-based technology measures are certainly stronger than the place-based measures. . . . We strongly confirm Putterman and Weil's (2008) seminal insight that history of peoples matters more than history of places.[5]

If you're trying to guess a nation's income per person in 2002, the migration-adjusted tech measure handily beats the migration-unadjusted measure. The relationship is always at least twice as strong, and the year 1500 migration-adjusted tech measure explains well over half of all cross-country income differences today. Over the last five centuries, for the world as a whole, it's fair to summarize economic history this way: the more things change, the more they stay the same—but only when you adjust for migration.

The New York Times Graph

This simple result has captured the attention of the *New York Times*: in 2010, its economics blog reported on this paper and printed its key figure, which shows that "migration-adjusted technology heritage" is a strong predictor of income per person in 2002. Catherine Rampell, then with the *Times* and now with the *Washington Post*, posed this question in the title:

Was Today's Poverty Determined in 1000 BC?[6]

And she posed part of her answer as a question:

So what if I told you that economic success was instead determined by what your ancestors did more than a millennium ago?

And while the history of "more than a millennium ago" doesn't appear to matter all that much for the present, what your ancestors did half a millennium ago seems to matter a lot, according to Rampell: "As it turns out, technology in AD 1500 is an extraordinarily reliable predictor of wealth today."

But look at the x-axis of a figure much the same as Rampell's (figure 3.1). Her x-axis was labelled "Migration-adjusted technology level in AD 1500." It's not the past of your *place* that's the "extraor-

FIGURE 3.1. The *New York Times* **graph revisited.** Migration-adjusted Technological History score (T) predicts 2005 income per person.

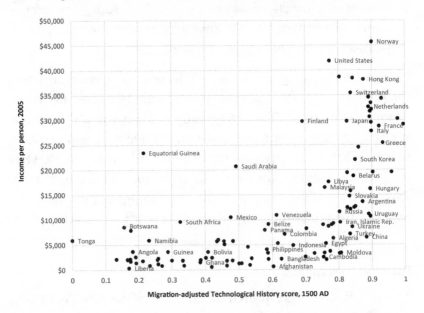

Sources: Comin, Easterly, and Gong (2010); Heston, Summers, and Aten (2006).

dinarily reliable predictor"; it's instead the "migration-adjusted" past, the past of the *people* who currently live in that place.

Comin, Easterly, and Gong are clear about how their results disrupt the standard narrative that the global poverty of today is overwhelmingly due to the very real, extremely brutal, post-1500, post-Columbus oppression. They note that the

> difference in per capita income today between Western Europe and sub-Saharan Africa is . . . a factor of 13.3. This income difference is usually attributed to the post-1500 slave trade, colonialism, and post-independence factors in sub-Saharan Africa. [But in Comin, Easterly, and Gong's simple model] 78 percent of the . . . difference in income today between sub-Saharan Africa and West-

ern Europe . . . is associated with the technology differences in 1500 AD.[7]

In sub-Saharan Africa as elsewhere, the pre-1500 past is prologue. For researchers who know the relative standing of pre-1500 technology in sub-Saharan Africa, the region's low income levels today come as, alas, little surprise. The great evils that others—Westerners and North Africans in particular—brought upon the region are almost surely an important cause of low productivity in that region. But they are unlikely to be the entire cause and perhaps not even most of it. It may well be that since scores for State History, Agricultural History, and Technological History are all relatively low for sub-Saharan Africa, we'd be best served by focusing our attention on the extremely distant past if we want to understand most of sub-Saharan Africa's poverty today.

Comin, Easterly, and Gong run the same kinds of horse races that Putterman and Weil ran, in order to see if there's a better horse than their three tech measures. In particular, they run races against simple geography measures: whether a nation is landlocked, how far it is from the equator (including whether there's a Goldilocks distance from the equator, neither too close to nor too far), and whether it's in the tropics. Once they run these races, the 1000 BC and 0 AD tech measures don't look that robust—raw geography beats them out—but the 1500 AD tech measure still does very well, a strong predictor of prosperity. And as we saw last time around, just because these geography measures predict prosperity doesn't mean that they're the entire reason they do well in the statistical race—correlation, causation, and all that. But it's good to have a little statistical sparring to see what works, and it's pretty clear that the year 1500 migration-adjusted tech index works.

Calculating a Nation's SAT Score

I've drawn attention to three major indicators that robustly link the past and the present:

S: State History since 0 AD

A: Agricultural History in thousands of years

T: Technological History since 1500

Let's combine these three measures into one handy index: a nation's migration-adjusted SAT score. You'll notice that I'm leaving out the urbanization measure—a very useful indicator of past productivity—as well as the 1000 BC and 0 AD tech index measures, which didn't do as well in the horse races. But "SAT score" is easier to remember than "SATU score," and it's smart to focus on the year 1500 tech measure because it captures something we all intuitively understand: European and East Asian strength in technology has persisted for five hundred years. Quite a track record, one not to be forgotten.

There are other measures of the distant past one could discuss—and we'll turn to a few in due time—but let's stick with the classics, the ones that created this still-growing scholarly literature. I'll convert the A score into a number running from 0 to 1 (0, newest to farming; 1, the oldest farmers, those near Iraq); with that, all three numbers will handily run from 0 to 1. Then I'll sum them up two ways, always migration-adjusted:

SAT: A simple average of the three scores, no hiding the ball.

SAT*: A "best-fit" weighting of the three scores, rigged[8] to do the best job possible of predicting income per person in every country around the world. One "best fit" for the whole world, so it's not artisanally crafted for each country. And it turns out, perhaps unsurprisingly, that the best fit is one that gives the vast majority of the weight to T, to migration-adjusted Tech History.

That extraordinary power of T to predict today's prosperity shows up when we look at Western Europe, a region slow to pick up on the settled farming lifestyle (modest A) but near the global technological frontier in 1500 (high T). Obviously, Western Europe is still near the economic frontier today, and the SAT* index, by giving a high weight to T, does a good job reflecting that strong link between T and modern prosperity.

And consider another apparent anomaly, where S and T tell different stories: Ethiopia. Ethiopia's essentially uninterrupted and deeply ancient history of organized statehood up to 1500 (with the highest possible value of S) doesn't do much to help us understand Ethiopia's current economic weakness, where average incomes per person today are around the 20th percentile of the global distribution. But Ethiopia's middling T score—nowhere near the world's lowest, but in the company of nations like Afghanistan, Burkina Faso, and Ecuador—makes Ethiopian poverty, sadly, less of a surprise and closer to a case of *plus ça change, plus c'est la même chose.*

The SAT and SAT* for each country are reported in the appendix, but let's look at a few in table 3.2, one for each major region of the world, and compare them to income per person.

While the SAT* scores rank up perfectly with income for these six countries, the simpler SAT scores don't. With just six countries, it's not too much of a surprise that we had a perfect SAT* fit. When we compare all the nations in the world together, SAT can predict 61 percent of (the logarithm of) cross-country income differences (not bad), but SAT* can predict 75 percent, three-fourths of cross-country income differences. That 75 percent is more impressive when you consider that this statistical analysis includes quite a few OPEC members, such as oil-rich Algeria, Iran, and Venezuela, nations that make much of their money the old fashioned-way—by pulling it out of the ground.

While we shouldn't dwell on every exception to SAT*'s strong predictive power, there are two big exceptions that I will pay attention to: the world's two most populous countries, India and China. Each has about 1.3 billion people, and together they contain a third of the world's population, so it's worth taking a moment to consider them both. Notice that China's SAT* score is almost at the level of Germany, but in 2002 it only had about one-sixth of Germany's income per person. And India in 2002 had about the same

TABLE 3.2. **SAT, SAT*, and national prosperity of six representative countries.** The SAT column is a simple average of migration-adjusted State, Agricultural, and Technological History scores. The SAT* column gives greater weight to Technological History, as described in the text and in greater detail in the appendix.

	SAT	SAT*	Income per person, 2002
Canada	0.72	0.87	$29,900
Germany	0.81	0.82	$27,200
China	0.90	0.78	$4,500
India	0.75	0.63	$2,600
Bolivia	0.50	0.33	$2,500
Cameroon	0.27	0.12	$2,000

Sources: Comin, Easterly, and Gong (2010); author's calculations.

average income as Bolivia, even though India's SAT* score is far higher. So, the world's only two nations with over a billion citizens are big exceptions to the global rule.

So, must we throw up our hands at these exceptions? No! We should instead notice that both nations are growing much faster than the average country in the world, and so both India and China are rising in the global rankings. When I'm teaching, I actually have to keep this in mind, since in just my two decades as a professor, China has gone from being the 124th richest country to the 72nd richest. And easy it's to see much of the reason: in the 1980s, both India and China went from being extremely hostile to competitive markets to being somewhat market-oriented, though both remain quite corrupt by global standards. But even that moderate shift away from anti-market hostility was enough to set off decades of growth. Every decade, both India and China are moving closer to where you'd predict based solely on their nation's SAT score. Every decade, India and China are becoming less of an exception, and each is moving closer to the rule. Those two fast-growing countries are heading right where they belong.

The Other Deep Roots Scores

SAT and SAT* aren't the epilogue to our story of how past is prologue. We've already seen that past urbanization can predict migration-adjusted national productivity today, and because scholars are endlessly creative, there are by now quite a lot of other measures of possible historical drivers of cross-country differences. The last two decades have been a gold rush for studying what's often called the "Deep Roots" of comparative economic development, the strong economic ties between past and present. One illustration: Brown University, home of Putterman and Weil, has long hosted an annual conference called "Deep Rooted Factors in Comparative Economic Development." (I went once; it was excellent.) As with any gold rush, there have been big strikes, big failures, and quite a few solid producers. Economists interested in the Deep Roots literature investigate claims that modern economies are bearing fruit planted centuries, even millennia, in the past. And some, but far from all of the Deep Roots research tests the claims of cultural transplant theory, the view that migration transplants economically important cultural roots from one land to another. Let's consider two of the more prominent successes of the Deep Roots literature: Genetic Distance and Genetic Diversity.

Enrico Spolaore of Tufts and Romain Wacziarg of UCLA have looked at the genetic distance between people in the richest countries and everyone else; they summarized their work in a paper whose title helped name the field: "How Deep Are the Roots of Economic Development?"[9] To create their Genetic Distance measure, they look at only what's known as "junk DNA," the parts of our DNA that don't code actual genes. They look at just the parts of human DNA that appear to collect and store, almost permanently, the genetic equivalent of typographical errors. If one of these typos were to wind up in one of the sections of DNA that actually contains the code for a specific protein, the typo would likely be damaging, so such DNA typos tend to get weeded out through normal Darwinian natural selection: broken DNA can't be fixed, so it usually gets thrown out. Of course, if one of those typos is a good one, the kind that turns lemons into lemonade, then it has a good chance of becoming more common over the centuries. But in the junk DNA sections, those typos accumulate like graffiti on the wall of an abandoned warehouse—once written, there forever.

My favorite metaphor for junk DNA: typos in medieval manuscripts. A standard way of figuring out where the original source of a medieval copy of, say, a New Testament manuscript came from is by looking at the pattern of typos. If a monk, patiently hand copying the Gospel of John, accidentally writes that "Paul came from back the dead," someone is guaranteed to catch such an obvious error and will fix it or discard that page. But if someone hand copying the same gospel accidentally writes that Jesus went "toward" Capernaum rather than "to" the town, that might slip past the quality-control officer. And when that manuscript is later recopied, there's a good chance the mistaken *toward* stays in. In the Middle Ages, there was a conservatism when it came to copying manuscripts: Keep copying the manuscript you have, as reliably as you can, and don't put too much effort into second-guessing minor changes in the manuscript. You probably don't have a version lying around that you're sure is better.

If you find a collection of manuscripts that all contain the phrase "toward Capernaum" and a few more rare errors in common, you can't be sure that those exact parchments were written by the same person, but you can be pretty sure they had the same *ancestor*, that they were each the copy, or the copy of a copy of a copy, of that first "toward Capernaum" manuscript. And here's my favorite part: you'll often find that quite a few manuscripts with the same sets of typos all exist within a particular region—say, all within about fifty miles of medieval Canterbury. Some were six miles to the north, some fifteen miles to the east, and quite a few fifty-five miles to the west. So, you might start guessing that the original typos came from Canterbury. The common set of errors is a clue to the origin of those errors.

The DNA copying process works much the same way: once a typo gets in, there's a good chance it'll get copied onto the next human manuscript, and the next one after that. And with 3 billion lines of DNA code, even a tiny, tiny rate of error in the junk DNA sections means there are a lot of typos that can identify where someone almost surely came from. The typos in junk DNA work a lot like a fingerprint: it doesn't matter what the fingerprint looks like; it just matters that yours and mine are different. But compared to fingerprints, DNA typos don't change much each generation—they change very, very slowly. That means that on average, people in Ireland typically have a different set of typos than people in France—and both have a quite different average set of typos than people in Japan. Since there are big global datasets that report these junk DNA typos for countries around the world, it's easy to measure how different people in one country are from people in others. And since the DNA typos accumulate at a roughly constant rate every generation, the amount of *difference* turns into a measure of historical *distance*. Groups that separated 10,000 years ago and had little later contact with each other (like, say, Africans and East Asians) have quite different sets of DNA typos. By contrast, people who separated less than 500 years ago (like, say, English people living in England and English Americans) will have only a few differences in their set of typos.

Spolaore and Wacziarg presumed that DNA typos are pointless, useless, and create no substantive differences between people. At the time they claimed that, it was a common view. Today, there's a lot of real debate over whether junk DNA is 100 percent junk or more like half-junk, half-important,[10] but fortunately that doesn't matter for Spolaore and Wacziarg's purposes. Like them, we'll treat these elements of DNA the way we treat fingerprint differences between two people—in other words, not important at all except when trying to ID a person.

Spolaore and Wacziarg created Genetic Distance measures using this junk DNA and asked whether nations that are genetically closer to the world's leading economy (the U.S.) are richer than countries that are more distant. They remind readers repeatedly that they're using these Genetic Distance measures not because they're convinced that Americans have genetic traits that cause prosperity—they're not trying to test that theory, not at all. Instead, they note that a key reason they're using the Genetic Distance measure is as an objective measure of cultural distance. And they think that when two cultures are similar to each other, it will be easier to pass good ideas (or bad ideas) back and forth. Cultural similarity, like half a glass of wine, helps people communicate. If your languages are pretty similar, if your ways of seeing the world are pretty similar, it's easier to share your culture's innovations with your neighbor's culture. But big cultural differences likely mean barriers to sharing ideas, whether it's a new joke that doesn't quite translate or a new way of arranging the assembly line that won't quite fit in with the norms of the distant, very different culture.

So, why not just measure cultural distance? Well, Spolaore and Wacziarg try that as well, using a well-known method: language similarity. And both the Language Distance measure and the junk DNA Genetic Distance measure tell a similar story: nations that are culturally or genetically closer to the U.S. are richer on average. But the Genetic Distance measure does far better at predicting prosperity.

So, that's one influential Deep Roots measure, a measure of Genetic Distance that's surely also an indirect measure of cultural distance. It's a little hard to be sure just why it works, but it certainly does work as a matter of raw power to predict modern prosperity. And it survives a lot of tire kicking: running Genetic Distance against climate measures or geography measures like whether a nation is landlocked or an island or asking whether Genetic Distance is just capturing the fact that some continents, on average, are richer than others. Genetic Distance does quite well in all of these contests. It's no surprise that their original paper was published in Harvard's influential *Quarterly Journal of Economics* and has been cited over seven hundred times in scholarly papers and books.[11] The work of Spolaore and Wacziarg has been an inspiration to other researchers in the area.

Brown University's Oded Galor and Quamrul Ashraf of Williams College came up with another theory of how the past could shape the present, and they likewise came up with another way to measure that past.[12] Their theory focused on comparing the benefits against the costs of cultural diversity. The benefits of cultural diversity are in part the benefits of a society that's made up of truly unique individuals who each have different strengths. Those diverse individuals can each focus on their individual strengths, yielding a whole that really is—no clichés here—greater than the sum of its parts. Back in 1776, the founder of economics, Adam Smith, told a related tale in his classic story of the pin factory, where one worker stuck to cutting the thin wire to the right length, another sharpened the wire tip to a fine point, a third flattened the other end slightly, and others packed the pins so that they could be sold by the hundred-count. Smith emphasized that if each worker stuck to the same job all day long, the whole team could produce pounds of pins per day—many thousands—but if each person had to do each step himself, he'd be lucky to produce a few dozen in a day. Smith rightly saw that greater specialization—greater job diversity—could help build modern prosperity.[13]

If Galor and Ashraf were to retell Adam Smith's story, they'd probably say that some people are better at wire cutting, some better at sharpening, some at boxing up, and so on—and the more diverse people are, the better the chance of someone being just fantastic at one pin factory job (even though he might be terrible at every other job in the same factory). In a world of diverse people, there's a better shot of finding just the right job that suits a person's skills. Adam Smith said that the division of labor is limited by the extent of the market (in a sense, by the size of the society). But Galor and Ashraf would be right to update Smith's theory: in addition, the division of labor is limited by the extent of a society's diversity of skills. In a wildly skill-diverse society, we can hope to pair the best-ever wire cutter with the best-ever wire sharpener, and the two of them together can make all the pins we'd ever need. It's a simple formula:

greater skill diversity +

a large, open society where the best can find each other =

massive increases in productivity and prosperity for just
    about everyone

That's one example—a symbol really—of the benefits of skill diversity. But there are costs of diversity as well, and they have something in common with Spolaore and Wacziarg's story about cultural
distance. In a diverse group, it might be hard to all get on the same
page, to organize complicated tasks, to get all the ducks in a row. If
we all have different visions that we can each work on separately—
each in our separate corner of the pin factory, as it were—then co-
ordination is unimportant. But often we have to agree on some big
tasks, or at least come together on them: maybe we have to agree on
which times of day to open and close the factory or on who has to
work weekends before Christmas or what to serve at the factory caf-
eteria. I intentionally picked low-conflict examples, problems that
can be hassles to solve but not deal breakers—because if there are
enough of those little hassles, they add up to a bad culture at work,
productivity is lost, and workers shirk at their jobs or quit.

There are more obvious examples of social conflict due to high
levels of diversity—there's a reason the phrase "ethnic conflict," a
topic of chapter 5, is a staple of daily newspapers and history books
alike. But even the smaller costs of diversity can be a barrier to efficiency, to productivity, to prosperity.

So far this is all just theory, just chit-chat with some hypothetical examples. But Galor and Ashraf didn't stop at the just-so-story
phase: they went out and collected data and tested their theory.
They found measures of the level of genetic diversity within different countries around the world, again drawing on the big cross-
country genetics datasets that are now everywhere. Their theory
predicted that there would be a Goldilocks level of genetic diversity
within each country: too little and you don't get many benefits of
diversity, too much and the social conflict costs of diversity wipe
out those benefits. A happy-enough medium would balance the

(falling) benefits against the (rising) costs of greater diversity within the society.

And sure enough, that's just what they found. It's well known that sub-Saharan Africa has the world's highest levels of genetic diversity within its boundaries. All modern humans are descendants of people who lived in Africa, and humans have lived far longer in Africa, especially sub-Saharan Africa, than anywhere else on the planet. That long period of time in Africa is one important reason why sub-Saharan Africans today are the most genetically diverse group of humans anywhere.[14] Small numbers of Africans who left that continent over the last 10,000 years became the ancestors of Europeans and Asians—and given their small numbers, they brought only a moderate amount of genetic diversity to the Eurasian landmass.

So, if sub-Saharan Africa has the most genetic diversity, and Eurasia has a moderate amount, which region has the least genetic diversity, the smallest opportunity to have near neighbors who are genetically a bit different? The Americas, before Europeans arrived. The Asian immigrants who came across the Bering Strait were few in number, and it appears they didn't bring that much genetic diversity by global standards—or at least those whose descendants survived and peopled the Western Hemisphere didn't have much genetic diversity by global standards. And today, the nations in Latin America that tend to be the poorest tend to be those with the largest percentage of Native American descent.

You'll notice that both the Genetic Distance story of Spolaore and Wacziarg and the Genetic Diversity story of Galor and Ashraf have something in common: both easily flip back and forth between "genetic" stories and "cultural" stories, and both are using the genetic evidence for what is at heart a cultural story.

But the two stories also have big differences. In the case of Genetic Distance, it's largely a story about cultural, economic, and social similarity to your neighbors in nearby countries, whereas in the case of Genetic Diversity, it's largely a story about cultural, economic, and social diversity within your nation. They really are distinct stories.

You might think it's now time to pick a winner among these measures, but that's not going to happen. I'm not going to come to a final conclusion on these many measures, not just yet anyway. There may well be something to all of them; prosperity is surely a recipe that can be made with many ingredients in different combinations. But I am going to point out this important fact: in all these cases, with all these measures of the past, whether it's

State History,

Agricultural History,

Technological History,

Past Urbanization Rates,

Genetic Distance from the economic frontier, or

Genetic Diversity within a nation—

in all of them, the migration-adjusted measure beats out the unadjusted one. If you're trying to predict a modern nation's prosperity in a part of the world that a lot of people have moved to since 1500, you definitely, absolutely, without a doubt want to pay attention to who has moved where.[15]

Let's also remember that if the extremely ancient past matters, it will matter for the less recent past, not just for today. Putterman and Weil made this point in their original paper. They used an early version of Comin's tech index and found that if you were trying to predict a nation's prosperity today, the year 1500 Technological History (T) beat out their ancient State and Agricultural History scores (S and A). They had a simple and likely correct explanation for that finding: the cultural traits that created past S and A scores ultimately shaped T scores in the year 1500: places with centuries of organized states and a long history of settled agriculture were likely, at least by the year 1500, to be using a lot of the world's best technology. That makes the tech index in 1500 a shorthand for past S, past A, and other past experiences that spurred a region to adopt the world's best technology.

So, it's useful to think of S and A as two of the ingredients in the T recipe. Or at the least, S and A are proxies, handy measures of persistent past success with complexity (important for life in organized states) and forward thinking (important for life amid settled agriculture), both of which are going to help create technological success. The extremely distant Deepest Roots are, in part, the parents of the later Deep Roots. S and A shape T, the most important single measure of the Deep Roots.

What If It's All a Coincidence?

In 2019, economist Morgan Kelly of University College Dublin released a paper that claimed that most of relationships I've covered in this chapter and the previous one might all just be a coincidence.[16] But fortunately, since he's an economist and not a television pundit, he didn't just claim it could be a coincidence; he actually made a case, offered some serious evidence, that it might just be a coincidence. The argument used some fancy statistics, but his main point is straightforward. Let me translate his key mathematical claims into English:

> There aren't as many countries in the world as you think there are.

> Why? Because most countries are near clones of their neighbors.

> So, if you see over a hundred countries that have a pretty strong relationship between an ancient Deep Roots score and modern prosperity, ask yourself if you would be much less impressed if it were just a handful of countries with such a relationship.

Indeed, when these papers use data from over a hundred countries, you might be impressed at first: what are the chances of State History doing such a good job predicting modern prosperity across over a hundred countries? If there were only three or four countries in the world, sure, any index might pick a winner a couple of times—a little like calling three out of four coin flips correctly. Nice, but not impressive; just randomly, you'd do that well 25 percent of the time. But consider one hundred coin flips: if you're calling at least seventy-five of them right, that's far, far better than random. Anybody who's correctly guessing at least seventy-five out of one hundred coin flips has a real knack, a real insight into coin flips: there's only around a one-in-a-million chance of doing that well by dumb luck.

Kelly claimed, essentially, that the only reason it looked like the Deep Roots measures predicted modern prosperity was that we thought we were flipping the coin a hundred times when we were flipping it only a handful of times. It was the statistical equivalent of an optical illusion. In reality, so many countries are so much like their neighbors that it's more like five or ten coin flips than like one hundred or two hundred. The point Kelly made had been made before, but he made the point much more thoroughly than other economists, and he backed it up with computer simulations. He pointed out that since most countries really are a lot like their neighbors in a lot of ways—"near clones" as I put it—then we're making a mistake if we think of there being one hundred separate pieces of evidence on the power of the past. Instead, it's more like having five or ten separate pieces of evidence—plus about ninety more pieces of evidence that are just blurry copies of the first five or ten. Think of there just being nine regions of the world:

> Europe
>
> South Asia
>
> Southeast Asia
>
> East Asia
>
> Oceania (including Australia and New Zealand)
>
> North America
>
> South America
>
> Sub-Saharan Africa
>
> Middle East + North Africa

Really, countries within these regions are often a lot like their closest neighbors. Within Europe, if you pick a Protestant country at random, most its closest neighbors are also probably Protestant. If you pick a European country that used to be in the Soviet bloc, good chance most of its neighbors were too. Think of almost any trait: whether people regularly eat salted fish, whether they are close to their extended family, or importantly for us, how much income the average person earns.

And of course, taking Europe as a whole, its cultural traits overall are quite different from, say, Southeast Asia taken as a whole. Countries are quite a lot like their near neighbors (when compared against the rest of the world), and countries within a region are typically quite different from those they are physically far from (with the obvious exceptions of migration-heavy countries such as Canada, the United States, and New Zealand). So, Kelly is right: we certainly don't have one hundred unique countries; we have a dozen, or at most a couple dozen, "typical" or "representative" countries in a region and then some near clones. Sorry, Canada: Homer Simpson was right, and you really are, from a statistical point of view, America Junior.

Kelly shows that for the kind of "near cloneness" we see on our planet, we'll probably find a lot of false positives, lucky coin flips, animal shapes in the clouds that really aren't there. Too many comparisons between the ancient past and the economic present will appear to be no coincidence at all; they'll look like something important, something "statistically significant." Hey, look, Protestant countries tend to drink less wine than Catholic countries—maybe it's the Protestantism that did that! Sounds plausible until we recall that Protestant countries are often near each other, and they're in climates too cool to grow good grapes. Proximity can create a lot of coincidences, which makes it harder to be sure that a pattern is real and not just a fluke. That's something that scholars should be concerned about, and indeed it's something that many of the papers in the area—especially those published in recent years—have tried to check for.[17]

But are these "animals in the clouds" likely to be a problem for the measures we've investigated in this chapter and the previous one? That's extremely unlikely. Why? Because the key trait we're interested in is always the *comparison* between the migration-adjusted scores and the migration-unadjusted scores. And as we've seen, there's absolutely no comparison: the migration-adjusted scores usually look great, and the migration-unadjusted ones usually look awful.

That's precisely the opposite of what Kelly's proximity theory would predict! If nations tended to have traits in common with their physically close neighbors, we'd find a lot of patterns like these: the U.S. would be a lot like Mexico, and Singapore (most of whose citizens are descended from Chinese immigrants) would be a lot like its near neighbor Malaysia (which received much less Chinese migration). But that's not what we find, not at all. In real life, if you want to predict modern prosperity in a high-migration country, it's much better to know the Deep Roots scores—SAT scores, urbanization rates, and so on—in the countries that nation's ancestors came from.

Kelly's theory predicts stronger *spatial* relationships, but cultural transplant theory predicts stronger *migration-adjusted* relationships. And by now, you know which theory is closer to the data: the Deep Roots tend to migrate—and as we've seen, cultural attitudes tend to migrate as well. And that's not at all what Kelly's "physical neighbor = near clone" theory predicts. Kelly's theory predicts that the migration-unadjusted measures should be the statistical winners, and the migration-adjusted measures should be the losers. Kelly's explanation is a theory that places, not people should predict prosperity, but reality shows that people matter enormously. Kelly's critique is interesting, and it's received a lot of attention, but ultimately it demonstrates the importance of the migration-adjusted Deep Roots of prosperity. And now that we've witnessed the power of migration-adjusted SAT scores to predict economic poverty and prosperity, we'll find that those migration-adjusted SAT scores also have the power to predict political corruption and political competence.

4 The Migration of Good Government

Little else is requisite to carry a state to the highest degree of opulence from the lowest barbarism, but peace, easy taxes, and a tolerable administration of justice; all the rest being brought about by the natural course of things.

—Adam Smith, 1755, as quoted by Dugald Stewart[1]

SOME PLACES HAVE BETTER GOVERNMENTS THAN others. In some countries, if you want to get your driver's license in a week rather than a year, you really ought to get a cash-stuffed envelope in the hands of the right government official. I'm told—for real, on good authority—that one doesn't just slide the envelope across the counter at the Motor Vehicles Department. That would be too crass. Instead, the first time you show up to the Motor Vehicles Department, you tell the person behind the counter that you'd like to get your license a little bit faster than usual, so the person behind the counter hands you a slip of paper with a phone number. When you call that number you're told when to show up at a certain address, an apartment actually, with the correct amount of cash in an unsigned envelope.

When you show up to the apartment, a man answers the door, takes your blank, cash-filled envelope, and tells you which day and which time you should go back to the Motor Vehicles Department. When you show up at the right time, your license is ready for you. And here's the best part: you don't even have to take the driving test.

Such low-grade corruption happens in many countries—bribery is often the only way to get things done in a lot of places—but it definitely happens more in some places than others. And as we'll see, it's more likely to happen if your nation's ancestors are from regions with low SAT scores.

Searching for the Deep Roots of Government Quality

One could well imagine that whatever it was that immigrants with long histories of state development took with them . . . manifests itself in better institutions or in a culture more favorable to economic success.

—Putterman and Weil, *Quarterly Journal of Economics*, 2010[2]

It's no surprise that in the first great paper on the Deep Roots, Putterman and Weil checked to see if State History was a good predictor of government quality (they skipped Agricultural History, but we'll see results for that soon). The link between good government and national prosperity seems obvious to many economists—and we have a strong hunch that it's mostly the good government causing the prosperity and not the other way around. Since theirs was the first paper on the topic, Putterman and Weil didn't run the most complicated, most thorough tests, but they did run the most important test: they checked whether the history of places mattered more than the history of peoples; they checked whether the deep roots of good government institutions tended to migrate. And migrate they did.

Let's look at their three measures of government quality. They picked these three because they were used in an influential paper coauthored by Harvard's Ed Glaeser[3]—a sign that they grabbed the best measures at hand rather than searching around and cherry-picking three measures that happened to make the Deep Roots of

State History look good. They chose "three indicators of institutional quality: executive constraints, expropriation risk, and government effectiveness."[4]

Executive constraints are a professor's way of restating the line by American Founding Father John Adams that "a republic [is] a *government of laws, and not of men.*"[5] In other words, executive constraints are rules that keep the leaders of the executive branch of government from doing whatever they like. And in turn that means using written law to restrain those with the power to tax and imprison from using that power to punish their foes and reward their friends.

Expropriation risk, Putterman and Weil's second measure, is the risk that the government will take stuff from citizens and businesses—perhaps by confiscating land or equipment outright or by seizing bank accounts, or maybe more subtly through surprise higher taxes and fees on political enemies, foreigners, and the very rich. Expropriation risk is the opposite of the right to property— that right enshrined in the U.S. Constitution's Fifth Amendment when it says, "No person shall be deprived of . . . property, without due process of law; nor shall private property be taken for public use without just compensation."

So, if you didn't break the law, then if the government is going to take your stuff without your permission, it has to pay you fair value. And this right to property goes back to Magna Carta, the great charter that King John was forced to sign at Runnymede in 1215. In Magna Carta, *we* refers to the king himself:

> No free man shall be . . . stripped of his rights or possessions . . .
> nor will we proceed with force against him, or send others to do
> so, except by the lawful judgment of his equals or by the law of
> the land.

And indeed, as economic historian Greg Clark notes in his excellent economic history *Farewell to Alms*, the risk of having your stuff taken by the monarch of Great Britain has been extremely low for centuries.[6] Some places have quite low expropriation risk—and at least so far, for most of the people most of the time, that low British risk has planted its Deep Roots in North America.

Government effectiveness, by contrast, is less about grand political debates, less about the proper scope of government, and more about making sure the trains run on time. The authors of the government effectiveness measure, Kaufmann, Kraay, and Zoido-Lobatón, drew on what Harvard's Glaeser and coauthors called "subjective assessments of institutional quality."[7] Kaufmann and coauthors said:

> In Government Effectiveness, we combine perceptions of the quality of public service provision, the quality of the bureaucracy, the competence of civil servants, the independence of the civil service from political pressures, and the credibility of the government's commitment to policies into a single grouping.[8]

Does the bureaucracy stand up to the politicians? Are the bureaucrats smart and do they show up on time? Are the government airports clean and functional? These are the kinds of "subjective assessments" that shape the government effectiveness measure.

Putterman and Weil check to see how State History predicts all three government quality measures. And State History works pretty well—as long as you adjust for migration. The migration adjustment matters a lot—yet another sign that people matter more than places. When you adjust for migration, the link between State History and expropriation risk gets twice as strong; for government effectiveness, the link gets three times as strong, and for executive constraints, four times as strong. Five centuries of migration appear to have mattered for government quality.

James Ang's Bigger, Tougher Set of Tests

The fact that migration-adjusted State History can do a decent job predicting modern government quality is important, but it's only the beginning of our inquiry. After all, we already know that State History loses out to Technological History when it comes to predicting a nation's income; State History is a noisy, ancient, simple measure of government quality. Indeed, the migration-adjusted measure of State History never explains more than a third of differences in government effectiveness—so it's surely not the whole story. But what is the whole story?

We'll never know the answer to that question—life always contains mysteries—but not for James B. Ang's lack of trying. An economist at Singapore's Nanyang Technological University, Ang wrote an astonishing 2013 paper, "Institutions and the Long-Run Impact of Early Development," a paper that grabbed just about every Deep Roots measure around and checked to see how they predicted modern government quality.[9] And of course, he made sure to check which mattered more: the Deep Roots of the place or of the people who today live in that place. I'll spoil the ending: for all of Ang's Deep Roots measures, the migration-adjusted measure did a better job predicting government quality than the migration-unadjusted measure. To paraphrase Putterman and Weil, when it comes to predicting government quality, the history of peoples matters more than the history of places.

The World Bank's Good Government Recipe

Ang uses one of the same government quality measures Putterman and Weil did: the government effectiveness measure created by World Bank researcher Daniel Kaufmann and his coauthors. However, that measure is just one of the six elements of what are known as the World Governance Indicators (WGI).[10] And while Putterman and Weil used just one element of the WGI, Ang also creates an average of all six of measures known as a "principal component," a sort of greatest-hits album based entirely on those World Bank measures.

Now, let's consider the other five elements of the WGI:

1. Regulatory quality—whether government rules make it easy for the private sector to function.

2. Rule of law—what you'd expect: "quality of contract enforce-
   ment, property rights . . . as well as the likelihood of crime
   and violence."

3. Control of corruption—both the buying-your-driver's-license
   kind and the buying-the-presidency kind.

4. Voice and accountability—a polite way of saying "democracy
   and freedom of speech in some form or another." The World
   Bank tries to be careful and speak in code on these politically
   delicate topics since it doesn't want to offend the undemocratic,
   repressive dictators and tyrants who sometimes fund them.
   And remember here as elsewhere in the WGI index, democracy
   and freedom of speech are matters of degree, not either-or.

5. Political stability—including absence of terrorism. A merely
   moderate chance of revolution can scare away a lot of investors and a lot of skilled would-be immigrants.

These all seem like good things, even though Voice and Accountability are a little hard to justify as a cause of prosperity per
se—although they are good in themselves! As I noted in my last
book, *10% Less Democracy: Why You Should Trust Elites a Little
More and the Masses a Little Less*,[11] the evidence that democracy
itself directly or indirectly helps increase national prosperity isn't
that strong. It may be more like a luxury good that rich countries
purchase, an effect more than a cause of prosperity.

But that's just one part of the six-part WGI index, so let's not
quibble. Instead, let's turn to Ang's seven Deep Roots measures.
You've already run across five of them:

State History

Agricultural History

Technological History

Genetic Distance from the U.S.

Population Density in 1500

The sixth is a nation's geographic distance from the richest country on the same continent; it's designed to capture the idea that great ideas diffuse slowly across long distances, that it's easier to learn from neighbors than from strangers. And after all of this, Ang creates a seventh Deep Roots measure: the first principal component of the other six, a fancy weighted average of them all. Let's call that seventh measure SAT+.

How do the seven rank as predictors of good government today? We'll only look at the migration-adjusted measures, since, as we know, they're the ones that really matter. In rank order, best to worst:

1. Technological History

2. SAT+

3. Population Density

4. Genetic Distance from the U.S. (a smaller distance is better)

5. Geographic Proximity to the regional economic leader in 1500 (again, a smaller distance is better)

6. State History

7. Agricultural History

And these differences between the top and the bottom of the list aren't small: Technological History does twice as good a job as Agricultural History at predicting good modern political institutions. The extremely ancient past, State and Agricultural History, each predict less than a third of modern differences across countries in government quality, while as figure 4.1 illustrates, Technological History in 1500 predicts 59 percent. If we took figure 4.1 literally— which you shouldn't—we'd conclude that while a national Tech History score of at least 0.7 doesn't guarantee higher quality governance, a score at least that high looks a lot like a prerequisite. Ang's SAT+ isn't far behind as a predictor, at 53 percent. By the way, when Ang checks to see how well these migration-adjusted Deep Roots scores predict income per person across countries, migration-adjusted Tech History wins again at 72 percent and SAT+ is in a close second at 64 percent, while State and Ag history are almost at the bottom, at 43 percent. Again, T wins the competition.

Ang doesn't stop there—once he establishes that Tech History and SAT+ are the winning predictors, he focuses most of his efforts on kicking the tires on those two measures. He checks to see if the power of these measures depends just on the "neo-Europes," the term that you'll recall economists use to refer to the U.S., Canada, Australia, and New Zealand, and a few other places. It doesn't. And it also doesn't depend on the inclusion of the region of the world with a highly disproportionate number of very poor countries, sub-Saharan Africa. If anything, dropping those thirty-three countries

FIGURE 4.1. Migration-adjusted Technological History score (T) predicts modern institutional quality. The institutional quality index is a simple average of the 2015 values of four of the World Bank's Worldwide Governance Indicators: Control of Corruption, Rule of Law, Government Effectiveness, and Regulatory Quality.

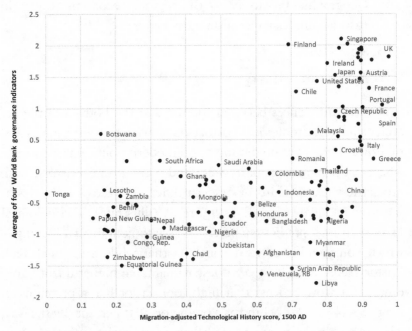

Sources: Comin, Easterly, and Gong (2010); Kaufmann and Kraay (2021).

in Africa makes these Deep Roots measures look a little more important. So, the poorest region and the big former British colonies in North America and Australasia don't appear to be driving these findings: instead, most of the world is telling most of our story.

Ang checks whether these two measures fall in importance if you already know a nation's current geography—the same measures we've seen, like latitude and whether it's landlocked or an island, plus a new one, terrain ruggedness—as well as other traits like the nation's religious background, education levels, which continent it's on, and a few other facts. When taken together, these extra features shave 40 percent off the predictive power of Tech History and 25 percent off the predictive power of SAT+. That means the relationship goes from astonishingly strong to just strong. Again, the migration-adjusted Deep Roots aren't everything, but they're a big part of the story—and they're being ignored in mainstream discussions of why some economies and some governments function better than others.

Ang asks one more important question: do Tech History and SAT+ matter for income directly, or do they only matter through their relationship with government quality? It's like asking whether a car's engine only matters because of what passes through the transmission, or whether the engine can somehow bypass the transmission and send energy directly to the car's wheels. In Ang's tests, it looks a lot like these two Deep Roots measures matter only through government institutions—or at least, the Deep Roots measures can predict modern prosperity only insofar as they can predict modern differences in government quality. According to Ang's results, the Deep Roots look a lot like an engine of prosperity, and that power runs solely through the transmission of government quality. If he's right, then people in every country should wonder how their nation's migration policies will shape the Deep Roots of their nation's government.

There Was No Reversal of Fortune (Adjusting for Migration)

In a 2002 paper, three famed economists, MIT's Daron Acemoglu and Simon Johnson and the University of Chicago's James Robinson, drew attention to a striking and (at least to we lazy economists) underappreciated fact: on average, when you look outside of Europe, the places that are the richest today were usually the poorest before 1500, and those that are the poorest today were usually the richest. North America is a classic example: Mexico, with its powerful, technically relatively sophisticated Aztec Empire, was far more prosperous than the areas we now call the United States and Canada. And South America captures the same fact: the Southern Cone, where relatively prosperous Chile, Argentina, and Uruguay exist today, was quite poor by regional standards.[12] And in the eastern hemisphere, Egypt and India had famously long histories of agriculture, sophisticated states, and technological expertise, while they are nowhere close to the global economic frontier today.

European colonization flipped the world's fortunes upside down, and Acemoglu, Johnson, and Robinson drew a conclusion: if colonization can reverse a nation's economic fortunes so completely, then prosperity isn't driven solely, or even mostly, by geography. As they put it: "Instead, the reversal in relative incomes over the past 500 years appears to reflect the effect of institutions . . . on income today."[13]

And in economics that view hasn't suffered a reversal of fortune over the last twenty years—instead, it has persisted. Acemoglu, Johnson, and Robinson argued that the reason colonized countries suffered a reversal of fortune was that colonizers brought good institutions to lightly populated countries (like the U.S. and Canada circa 1500) and brought bad institutions to heavily populated countries (like Mexico and Egypt). However, other economists, noticing who moved where since 1500, saw much less evidence for a reversal of fortune and more evidence for the Deep Roots theory of prosperity. A key example: a paper by Areendam Chanda of Louisiana State along with C. Justin Cook of the University of California at

Merced and the same Louis Putterman we've met before. Together, they showed that this apparent reversal of fortune—with Mexico moving down the rankings after 1500, the areas north of Mexico moving up the rankings—can be entirely explained by the fact that in the New World, lightly populated areas were often invaded by large numbers of migrants from countries with high SAT scores. By contrast, more heavily populated areas were, well, too heavily populated for invaders to displace the original inhabitants. The title of the paper says it all: "Persistence of Fortune: Accounting for Population Movements, There Was No Post-Columbian Reversal."[14]

The invaders destroyed many wonders, but they didn't ruin economies that had been destined to succeed. Instead, in nations that had been lightly populated beforehand, they raised national SAT scores, planting Deep Roots of economic institutions that would bear fruit ages later.

"Institutions matter" is a cliché now in economics, and so the grand questions turn not on whether government institutions matter but on why government institutions aren't equally good everywhere. And together, the evidence we saw in chapter 1 for cultural persistence among the descendants of immigrants and the evidence we've seen in this chapter that centuries-old migration-adjusted SAT scores predict modern government quality add up to a consistent story that migration shapes government quality in somewhat predictable ways.

It's time to say it out loud: the cultural transplant theory of government institutions does a good job, on average, of explaining differences in government quality across countries. It's entirely reasonable to believe that when it comes to the forces shaping government quality, peoples matter more than places.

5 Our Diversity Is Our _____

A body of literature suggests that ethnic heterogeneity limits economic growth.

—Jonas Hjort (Columbia University),
Quarterly Journal of Economics, 2014[1]

IF YOU'RE BUYING CUT FLOWERS in Europe, there's a good chance those flowers were grown, cut, and even arranged in Kenya. Kenya is home to a massive export-driven flower industry—around the third biggest in the world[2]—an industry that makes Valentine's Day possible every year. That industry draws on workers from multiple ethnic groups—multiple *tribes*, the term used locally—who are often in conflict with one other. And this ethnic conflict is so powerful that it is able to defeat one of the most powerful forces in the known universe: individual self-interest.

Economist Jonas Hjort wrote an influential paper on ethnic conflict in the Kenyan flower industry as part of his 2012 UC Berkeley doctoral dissertation, and he eventually published it in the Harvard-run *Quarterly Journal of Economics*. At the large Kenyan flower factory that Hjort studied, one worker is the "supplier" who brings in flowers from the greenhouse. The supplier then delivers flowers to two workers who are "processors," whose job it is to clean off the flowers, trim the stems, and package the flowers for delivery. So, one supplier gives flowers to two processors. At the firm Hjort studied, the work force, both suppliers and processors alike, was overwhelmingly comprised of two major ethnic groups: the Kikuyu (and their allied tribes) and the Luo (and their allied tribes). These two groups overwhelmingly vote for different political parties in government elections, just one signal of their deep disagreements, their ethnic conflict.

Workers typically stay on for about two and a half weeks at a time and then take an average of two days or three days off before coming back. When a worker goes on leave, the replacement worker may be Kikuyu or Luo—the firm doesn't assign jobs based on ethnic affiliation, so the replacement worker's tribe is a flip of the coin. That means that about half the time, the two processors are from the same ethnic group and half the time they're from different ethnic groups. So, when the two processors are from different ethnic groups, does the underlying ethnic conflict hurt worker productivity, or do they shrug off their ethnic differences when there's work to be done?

Drawing on data from over 900 workers combined into over 28,000 different teams, Hjort reports that in 2007, when the two processors were from different ethnic groups, they were 5 percent less productive than ethnically homogeneous pairs—and productivity dropped by 8 percent when the supplier and the processors were from different ethnic groups. In that place, at that time, ethnic diversity was not a strength. In that place, at that time, ethnic diversity was a weakness.

And here's what makes that finding striking: the workers were paid a piece rate, so essentially they were paid by the flower. More flowers, more money. These weren't salaried workers, slacking a little bit here and there but being paid the same amount regardless of how hard they worked. Doing a worse job meant taking home less pay—so this ethnic conflict took a direct hit on their wallets.

At the end of 2007, Kenya had a presidential election won by the Kikuyu candidate Mwai Kibaki. But the election's fairness was "disputed by the [Luo-led] opposition and the international community,"[3] not least because the Luo candidate, Raila Odinga, had been leading in opinion polls. Hjort describes the result:

> Widespread violence against Kikuyu and Kikuyu-allied tribes erupted, and counterattacks soon followed. More than 1,200 people were killed and 500,000 displaced in the months that followed. . . . It was not until after April 3 that the political crisis ebbed when the two sides reached a [power-sharing] agreement.[4]

How did this deadly political conflict shape work at the flower plant? By hurting the productivity of ethnically diverse teams even more than usual—but slightly boosting the productivity (and so the pay) of ethnically homogeneous teams. Kenya's political violence doubled the productivity gap between diverse and homogenous teams. So, the costs of ethnic diversity and the benefits of ethnic homogeneity aren't fixed—they can rise or fall as social tensions rise and fall. But at least in Kenya, the costs and the benefits were there for any statistician to behold.

Hjort makes every effort to drive home this particular point: workers are willing to hurt their own individual pay in order to lower the pay of someone in another ethnic group. This job requires a team effort—with the suppliers and processors working together to prepare and package the bundled flowers. So, when you're not helping the team, you're hurting yourself. And workers clearly hurt themselves: "Workers are willing to accept lower own pay to lower the pay of non-coethnic co-workers."[5]

That's shooting yourself in the foot in the hope that the bullet will fly through your wound and hit your enemy—a choice that is all too human.

Even when ethnic hostility is expensive, some people are willing to buy it. Of course, one could spend more time documenting the historical reasons for ethnic hostilities in this or that country during this or that era—and write dissertations and create Netflix documentaries on which side is mostly or totally to blame in different cases. But from the point of view of understanding national peace, national prosperity, national human flourishing, the most important fact to remember is that there will always, alas, be reasons for ethnic hostilities in many, many nations.

With enough time, with enough prosperity, and perhaps with the right cultural institutions, some ethnic distinctions can fade into near-irrelevance. Cultural differences between regions of France shrank over the centuries—they were a theme in Balzac's nineteenth century novels—and ethnic hostility between German Americans and English Americans, once so important in the mid-nineteenth century, now sounds more like a *Saturday Night Live* sketch than a social problem. But given how little we know about curing ethnic conflict, we should treat the conflicts we see as problems to live with for the long run.

A Perfect Test of a Terrible Problem

If we're trying to find out if greater ethnic diversity is, all things considered, good news or bad news, why would we look to Kenyan flower factories for evidence? Because most of the time, in most other research on ethnic diversity, it's hard to tell whether a problem is truly caused by ethnic diversity or instead is just accompanying ethnic diversity.

Consider a baseball team, the New York Yankees, that's looking to find a few new players. If the Yankees (a team with twenty-six players) decided to recruit a dozen second-graders for the team, that would increase the "age diversity" of the Yankees, and obviously this new version of the Yankees would perform abysmally against other Major League Baseball teams (though they'd still beat the Mets). So, a naïve observer might think it was the "rise in age diversity" that caused all of the lost games, but really it was the fact that they brought on a bunch of kids who just weren't very good at baseball.

A lot of tests of whether an increase in ethnic diversity is good news or bad are set up pretty much the same way: in a culture where one ethnic group is the overwhelming majority—and where the majority group is better-educated and richer than average—researchers check whether adding members of a typically less-educated and typically poorer ethnic group hurts average team performance. A "test" like that can't tell us whether worse group outcomes are due to the rise in diversity or due to the fall in average skill levels.

All the research we looked at in chapters 1–4 showed us how immigration can change a nation solely by changing the *average* traits of a nation's citizens. If a country with a low average Tech History score welcomes a lot of immigrants from nations with high average Tech History scores—as with the Chinese immigration thought experiment from the preface—then it's reasonable to guess that in a few decades that country will have better technology, higher incomes, and, eventually, less-corrupt government. And that's all true despite the fact that this immigration wave raised the "Tech History diversity" of the country!

Imagine a company that has workers from exactly two different ethnic groups. To really see if a rise in ethnic diversity—or cultural diversity or religious diversity—will tend to help or hurt group outcomes, we'd want to check how members of each group perform when they're working only with members of their own group, and then compare that performance against what happens when members of those different groups are working together. We'd like to treat the two homogenous groups as the *control* groups, the placebo groups, and then we can compare them against the diverse *treatment* group, the experimental group.

That's just what Hjort's Kenyan database lets him do: he can see how productive an all-Luo team is, how productive an all-Kikuyu team is, and then see how productive a team is when it combines some Luo and some Kikuyu members. Even better—since the very same 900 or so workers move between teams, he can check to see how the very same worker performs when she's with someone from her own ethnic group versus with someone from the other ethnic group.

And Hjort's evidence is clear: all-Luo and all-Kikuyu teams perform about equally well. There's no Luo advantage, no Kikuyu advantage. Each ethnic group is about as productive as the other when they're with just members of their own ethnic group. But when Luo and Kikuyu workers are working side by side, in pairs, output falls about 5 percent during times of relative peace, but about 9 percent during times of violent conflict.

This will be the kind of evidence we want to see when investigating whether ethnic diversity helps, hurts, or doesn't matter at all for group outcomes: a control group to compare against the treatment group. We want to know that when diversity increases, we can be fairly sure that any change in outcomes is *caused* by the diversity and not just *accompanied* by it. This opens the door to answering truly interesting and important questions like the following:

> If more ethnic diversity itself is bad in a certain case, is that because one specific ethnic group is causing the damage, or is this misery truly a team effort? Hjort's study clearly shows that in the flower factory he studied, the team-effort theory was true.

> To reverse the story, is it the reaction of others to one specific ethnic group that is causing the problem? Many explanations of modern racism place great weight on this particular theory of ethnic conflict: the majority's behavior toward the minority is the central focus.

> Is there a practical, non-utopian way to overcome, to eliminate the costs, the frictions of ethnic diversity? Are there real cures from mainstream social science, or is it all just alternative medicine?

Let me begin with an example from pure economic theory of when greater diversity per se is a benefit, full stop. It's a case that matters a lot in real life, and it illustrates a practical path to make diversity work. Suppose that during a deep recession, your company needs to hire a new worker. Since the economy is so bad, any person you make an offer to is almost sure to take the job. Obviously, you want to find the best person, so you're willing to search through an (electronic) pile of resumes to find her. There are two websites where you can post the job:

Mediocreville, where just everyone who uploads a résumé is pretty close to average.

Diversityville, where half the applicants are way above average and half are way below average—half superstars; half also-rans.

So, which website are you going to use to search for a new worker?

You can see where this is going: since you get to look at the job applications before you decide to whom to make the offer, it's smart to sign up for Diversityville, screen out the below-average applications, and only interview the superstars. When you're picking one applicant to make an offer to, and you can screen out the also-rans, all that matters to you is the upside. And that means that you'll be spending quite a few hours on Diversityville, quickly deleting the résumés that look below average and focusing on those that are above average.

The lesson? The power to filter, the power to screen boosts the power of diversity.

This commonsense idea draws on the work of Nobel laureate Joseph Stiglitz in a coauthored paper, building on the work of another Nobel laureate, George Stigler, and well known from a textbook authored by a third Nobel laureate we've already run across, Thomas Sargent.[6] Three other economics Nobel laureates have received their prizes in this general area[7]—known as search theory—and all the work points in the same direction: even when searching for new additional employees is costly—in time and money—as long as the better workers aren't much pickier than average about turning down jobs, more diversity in the job application pile is great news for the employer.

I think this is a big part of the reason why "diversity" polls so well among elites, and why elites often treat doubts about diversity as puzzling if not obviously immoral. Elites are much more likely than the average person to be in a position to screen, to filter, to check the Yelp ratings and résumés and standardized test scores and all the rest. They can screen out most of the possible costs of diversity and get most of the possible benefits.

When a list contains lots of options—restaurants you like and restaurants you're not in the mood for, to give an example—and you can afford to eat at any restaurant on the list, then why not have a diverse list of restaurants to choose from? Who could object to that? The options that aren't a good fit for you might be a good fit for someone else, and anyway, the option you don't choose is an option that isn't your problem.

When you're rich enough to screen out all the possible costs of diversity, all that's left are the cases where our diversity is our strength.

The Troubled Business Case for Ethnic Diversity

If our ethnic diversity is our strength, if ethnic diversity helps groups get more or better things done—or at least gets the same amount of work done in less time—then the greedy capitalists should be the ones to know about it. Businesses love to make a profit, the bigger the better. So, if ethnic diversity per se gives a boost to innovation or cooperation or any other part of a firm's profitability, we can expect businesses to exploit that profit opportunity to the maximum. You don't have to pass government mandates or quotas or "hiring targets" to get a company to take steps to boost its profits—a company will do what it takes to boost profits all by itself.

So, is there a "business case for diversity"? It depends on what you mean by *diversity*—and remember, on controversial topics, you should be on the lookout for loose language, obfuscation, and opaque jargon, especially in academic research. My fellow professors usually try hard to stay politically correct, and we'll often torture the definitions of words to try to stay PC. It turns out there really is a very good case to be made for "skill diversity," for creating work teams where different people have different skill sets. A lot of reality-show projects are like this—if you're remodeling an entire home in a week, you need a plumber and an electrician and someone with good design sense and a manager to keep all the ducks in a row. Fortunately, a lot of modern business tasks have a lot in common with those reality shows: if you're designing a new computer (a story well told in the 1981 classic *The Soul of a New Machine*[8]), you need some people who are great at coding and some at debugging and some at making sure the computer chips are far enough apart on the assembly board so that they don't overheat. There's a lot of evidence that skill diversity, in and of itself, gives a boost to performance.

I call that "*Firefly* diversity," after Joss Whedon's excellent, short-lived TV science fiction show about a gang of misfits with unusual skills who work together to help the human race. Oddballs every one: the pilot, the captain, the courtesan, the mechanic, the doctor, and (because it's Whedon) the young woman with a difficult past who is exceptionally good at martial arts. A lot of ensemble-cast movies use that trope:

> In the first act, we learn about a group of misfits with unusual skills.

> In the second act, the misfits start fighting with each other instead of against the Final Boss

> In the third act we have a Learning Moment, and then everyone works together to beat the Final Boss.

And yeah, the first two Avengers movies, classics of the fight-your-team-then-fight-the-enemy genre, were directed by Whedon. But *Star Wars: A New Hope* fits that pattern too, with Leia, Luke, and Han squabbling before they all come together to help vaporize the innocent political prisoners held on the Death Star. It's exciting to watch diversity turn into a strength, with each hero using unique special powers to finally defeat the Big Bad. But movies aren't reality—and in reality, only *some* kinds of diversity appear to be a strength. Skill diversity: that's one kind that appears to be a win for the team. Work out the kinks early, and then press on to victory.

What about the other kinds of diversity? The most famous overview of diversity in the workforce is perhaps by Kathryn Williams of Columbia University and Charles O'Reilly of Stanford, published back in 1998.[9] They looked at age diversity, sex diversity, ethnic diversity, *Firefly* diversity, and tenure diversity (how long a person has been at the company). Today's serious scholarly discussions about the effects of diversity in the workforce tend to begin with this paper. Williams and O'Reilly looked back at four decades of research in the area—back to the late 1950s—and found this:

> The preponderance of the empirical evidence suggests that diversity is most likely to impede group functioning. Unless steps are taken to actively counteract these effects, the evidence suggests that, by itself, diversity is more likely to have negative than positive effects on group performance.[10]

That bit about "unless steps are taken" makes you wonder if there are practical, implementable steps a business can take to turn diversity into a net strength. Or is this more like saying, "Unless steps are taken, exploding fireworks held in the hand are extremely dangerous"? Williams and O'Reilly don't offer any clear answers on that. Instead, you get the usual set of vague suggestions that "may" work:

> Organizational culture . . . may be a powerful way . . . to encourage solidarity rather than divisiveness.[11]

> Making salient the potential negative effects of social categorization . . . may encourage individuals to be aware of the possibility of discrimination.[12]

> Understanding these negative effects [of diversity] may provide a solution for its more pernicious effects.[13]

Makes you wonder if bracing yourself against the steering wheel "may" prevent injuries during a car crash. Maybe, if you're strong enough! At another point, they sum it up this way:

The evidence suggests that, by itself, diversity is more likely to have negative than positive effects on group performance. Simply having more diversity in a group is no guarantee that the group will make better decisions or function effectively.[14]

And at the same time, they note that a lot of the successes of diversity found in prior research had been cases of *Firefly* diversity:

Much of the literature that supports the claim that diversity is beneficial is often based on variation in individual attributes such as personality, ability, and functional backgrounds, and not on ascriptive attributes such as ethnicity and sex.[15]

In the early 2000s, another review came to a similar, perhaps more optimistic but noticeably vaguely worded conclusion:

The evidence that supports the often-made claim that *racio-ethnic diversity* improves performance is limited. One study found no significant relationship. . . . Some studies reported negative effects of racio-ethnic diversity on performance.[16]

A 2007 review in the prestigious *Annual Reviews* came to a similarly incomplete conclusion, looking at all forms of diversity in the workforce: "Evidence for the positive effects as well as for the negative effects of diversity is highly inconsistent."[17]

And a 2005 paper by Elizabeth Mannix of Cornell and Margaret Neale of Stanford took an even stronger position on overall diversity in the workforce:

The preponderance of the evidence favors a more pessimistic view: that diversity creates social divisions, which in turn create negative performance outcomes for the group. Why is the reality of diversity less than the promise?[18]

That's a great question, isn't it? And they summed up one paper that ran four separate studies this way: "Racial diversity tended to have negative effects on team process."[19]

By the 2010s business researchers were finally able to state it clearly: "Research and practice has found the business case for diversity to be elusive."[20] And the team that wrote those words summed up another era of scholarly research into diversity in the workforce—both ethnic and otherwise. Drawing on data from studies run around the world, they reported "no overall relationship between diversity and performance or a very small negative effect."[21]

And finally, a team of professors in the Netherlands, in the course of showing that ethnic diversity itself was a predictor of slightly weaker team performance, summed up the way scholars tend to talk about the issue today: "Indeed, it has become a truism that diversity is a double-edged sword."[22]

That phrase, "diversity is a double-edged sword," has caught on in business scholarship circles, and it's still in wide use, as you can confirm with a quick Google search.[23] The metaphor is well-chosen. There are some ways to use diversity as a strength—*Firefly* diversity, true skill diversity, has a lot going for it—but the costs are equally sharp and maybe more dangerous to the person trying it out. Professors use that phrase all the time; we'll know that our public debate over diversity has moved in the direction of the scholarly evidence when elected public officials can use the phrase as well.

Especially since social scientists lean so heavily to the political left,[24] the willingness to report these "double-edged sword" findings is an especially strong sign that at least in the heavily studied business world, it's hard to make the case that our diversity is, overall, our strength. No effect—or maybe a negative effect—should be our starting point for further serious discussion. That means that when you see people chanting, "Our diversity is our strength," you're hearing the cultural equivalent of second marriages: a triumph of hope over experience.

The Best-Case Scenario: Not Great

If diversity, including ethnic diversity, is a risky "double-edged sword" even when corporations can choose whom to hire and whom to fire, that should raise our concern that greater ethnic diversity will be riskier when we're talking about citizenship and permanent residency. Corporations can decide which job applicants are likely to be good at dealing with diversity, and they can ignore the job applications from people who they think might have a tough time adjusting to coworkers from different cultures. If big corporations can't routinely turn ethnic diversity into a strength—when they can try to hire good team players and fire the bad team players—what hope is there for a nation, a country, filled with whoever is on the citizenship rolls?

That's why I led with a study of ethnic conflict on the job. That's the best-case scenario for ethnic diversity in teams, and that best-case scenario, while obviously not a disaster to run away from at full speed—the flower teams in Kenya were only a few percentage points less productive when full-blown ethnic riots were going on elsewhere—is nothing to recommend. As a recent article in the *Harvard Business Review* said it, right in the title: "Getting Serious about Diversity: Enough Already for the Business Case."[25]

The Supply-Side Demand for Ethnic Diversity

In passing, I should note one fairly strong case for hiring a diverse workforce: when your customers are ethnically diverse, it's widely considered a good idea to have a workforce that's similarly ethnically diverse. This has been studied heavily in retail industries— and it looks like it's a good idea to have workers and members of the corporate board who have a lot in common with a company's customers. Knowing your customers is part of knowing how to serve your customers, and one way to know your customers is to have some workers and some board members who share the cultural background of your customers. This is one case where simple common sense turns out to be basically right.

But notice: this is a supply-side demand for diversity, an argument that you need to hire people from a variety of cultural backgrounds precisely because your company's customers are from that same variety of cultural backgrounds. A *supply* of diverse customers creates a *demand* for diverse workers. This isn't an unconditional argument that "our diversity is our strength," an argument that ethnic diversity inside the corporation will spur new ideas, create more innovation, improve corporate culture in general. Instead, the supply-side demand for ethnic diversity is the claim that for a variety of reasons, Korean employees help a company do well with Korean customers, Italian employees help a company to reach Italian customers, and so on.

But the supply-side demand for ethnic diversity means that a company needs diversity inside because the nation has diversity outside. Again: good common sense. But retail firms selling in Japan don't need that many French-speaking employees, precisely because there are so few French speakers in Japan. With Japan's small supply of diverse customers, there's much less demand in Japan for diverse workers.

Of course, the same supply-side demand for a diverse workforce that shows up in retail shows up in government agencies as well, especially for agencies that interact with the public: police, firefighters, schoolteachers, university professors. When a government agency has culturally diverse clients and customers and students and people in need of emergency assistance, there's an excellent case for hiring a culturally diverse workforce so that government employees can do their jobs more effectively.

But notice: again, this is a supply-side demand for diversity. And again, notice: the case rests crucially on the claim that multiculturalism, sustaining a culturally diverse society, is hard. The supply-side demand for diversity presumes (often correctly) that there's some barrier, some friction, some difficulty in having an employee from one culture provide high-quality services to a customer or client from another culture. The supply-side demand for diversity is built on the case that diversity needs to be handled well to succeed—it's another version of diversity as a "double-edged sword."

The Consultant's Case for Diversity

If diversity, particularly ethnic diversity, really is a double-edged sword as many researchers say, then why is there so much corporate-consultant happy talk about diversity being an obvious strength, a path to profits, a route to success? There are a lot of possible explanations, of course—maybe they just want to accentuate the positive. But perhaps it's a path to generate more consulting dollars: "Take an edge off the double-edged sword of diversity for the low price of $2,000 per billable hour per consultant!"

But often, the corporate consulting world isn't directly disagreeing with the kind of evidence we've covered in this chapter. All the evidence I've presented in this chapter has focused on conventional employees—workers, not top executives and certainly not members of the corporate board. The corporate consulting world, however, frequently likes to talk about pushing for greater demographic diversity—more women, more people of color—on corporate boards and among the top ranks of executives. And here, they at least have some recent history on their side; it really is the case that corporate boards with greater ethnic diversity tend to be more profitable than average. That doesn't mean the diversity caused the profitability, since activists will likely focus their efforts on the most profitable firms when pressing for greater representation for people of color: it could be simple reverse causation.

You know the old line attributed to bank robber Willie Sutton: Why did he rob banks? Because that's where the money was. Little point in pushing for seats on the boards of unprofitable companies. But I don't think that's the whole story, and maybe it's none of the story. I think this is a case where good old-fashioned forward causation is most of the story: a diverse board is a sign your firm is looking hard for the best people, including the best outsider perspectives. But first, let's see what consulting megafirm McKinsey has to say about the link between corporate profits and demographic diversity in top corporate jobs:

Correlation does not demonstrate causation.

McKinsey research established a statistically significant correlation—without claiming a causal relationship—between greater levels of diversity in company leadership and a greater likelihood of [higher] profitability.

And once more for the kids in back:

Correlation is not causation. While not causal, we observe a real relationship between diversity and performance that has persisted over time and across geographies.[26]

So, all we have is a correlation, a reliable historical pattern, between a more diverse corporate leadership and more corporate profits. That doesn't prove that the diversity caused the profits—again, it could be the reverse—but it's already a far stronger, more reliable pattern than we've seen between rank-and-file employee diversity and business success. And I think much of the story is that corporate leadership benefits from having a bigger pool of excellent people to draw from. Top corporate leadership jobs can always draw from the best of the best: it's common for pathbreaking professors, former senators, and retired military officials to sit on corporate boards, so top corporate jobs are drawing from many different parts of the global elite. In settings like this, vetting standards are high and most of the people being considered are already known quantities—they're friends of friends, coworkers of coworkers. This kind of mega-screened hiring pool is a far cry from flower processing plants of Kenya, a Texas middle school, or a French auto factory.

So far, that's one reason to suspect that when selecting for elite corporate jobs, greater demographic diversity is at least not a tax, not a source of friction. But we can say more than that. If a company searches for a diverse pool of top talent, it's almost surely searching in a bigger pool. If one Japanese company is searching for board members only among Japanese men, and another Japanese company in the same industry is also searching for similarly qualified Japanese women, along with top Korean, Taiwanese, and American executives who speak some Japanese, that second Japanese firm will have a bigger hiring pool. And a bigger hiring pool means a better chance of finding the best person for the job. Maybe it'll still turn out that a Japanese guy is the right person for the job in both cases—but looking further afield is smart, prudent, selfish, and a sign of a healthy corporate culture.

But there's another reason to think that at least in the 2020s, a more diverse top corporate team will cause a firm to become better: a diverse team is more likely to include corporate outsiders. And if there's one unambiguously robust result from corporate finance research, it's that corporations with more outsiders on their boards—people who never worked for the firm and who aren't related to anyone working for the firm—tend to do a better of pushing out bad executives. Insiders, friends and coworkers of a failing CEO, can always come up with a reason to give him "one more try," but an outsider on the board, a near stranger, is a lot more willing to have the failing CEO walk the plank.

Nobel laureate Jean Tirole noted this in his classic textbook *The Theory of Corporate Finance*,[27] and it's a theme throughout research into corporations: having outsiders, independent viewpoints, on the board is a great idea. Yes, it can go too far—you want some people on the board who know the firm well, which means insiders and industry experts are going to be valuable—but it's a safe bet that overall, getting some new ideas in the room, when those new ideas are provided by some of the world's most talented people, is likely to pay off.

The case of corporate leaders is another reminder: If you're in the elite, it's pretty likely that our diversity is our strength. But for the rest of us, that's still up for debate.

Whom Can You Trust?

Harvard's Robert Putnam has been studying trust and social bonds for decades. His most famous book is *Bowling Alone*—a classic from 2000 still well worth reading—where he showed that the social bonds of Americans have been fraying for decades.[28] His classic example was the bowling league—Americans used to belong to small-scale, local community organizations like bowling leagues and the Boy and Girl Scouts and joined social clubs like the Elks and the Freemasons, but over time those organizations have been in decline, replaced by TV and now by social media. He's right: people just don't meet their neighbors as much as they used to, and they're more socially isolated from the near strangers we call "our local community." It's not that people bowl less; it's that they're bowling alone.

Later, Putnam turned his attention to measuring social trust, drawing on the same kinds of survey measures we looked at in chapter 1. He wanted to find out what predicted more trust and what predicted less trust. And he found out that one strong predictor of whether you, as an individual, were trusting of others was whether you were in an ethnically diverse neighborhood: the higher the local diversity, the lower the trust. It was a striking result, a strong result, and a result he kicked the tires on to see if it was just the statistical equivalent of an optical illusion.[29]

But it survived the tire-kicking—and it's not just the kind of Yankees-hire-some-second-graders sort of fall in average trust. Yes, on average, Hispanics and Blacks in the U.S. are less trusting than whites, a result that's been widely documented, but the lower trust in diverse neighborhoods is still there even accounting for that. Let's make it concrete: in the typical neighborhood that was a 50–50 mix of a high-trust ethnic group and a low-trust ethnic group, the level of trust wouldn't just be halfway between the typical nationwide trust levels for those two ethnic groups: it's usually lower than that. It's a little like the Kikuyu and the Luo workers when they were placed on the same shift: being together made them each at least a little bit worse than otherwise.

Putnam gave his 2007 paper an ironic title, based on the Latin motto of the United States that I'll loosely translate as "out of many comes unity": "*E Pluribus Unum*: Diversity and Community in the Twenty-First Century." The title is closer to a hope than a finding: Putnam, a prominent Ivy League social scientist, wasn't quite sure whether diversity and community were going to coexist in this century.

That paper spurred endless responses; the question of whether greater ethnic diversity hurt trust had been studied before, but Putnam put it on the front burner. In 2020, a team at University of Copenhagen and at Aarhus University looked at 1,001 statistical estimates on ethnic diversity and trust from eighty-seven different studies from many rich countries. They published their results in the prestigious *Annual Review of Political Science.* The authors found that Putnam's result wasn't just the story of America; it was a global story:

> We find a . . . negative relationship between ethnic diversity and
> social trust across all studies. The relationship is stronger for trust
> in neighbors, and when studied in more local contexts.[30]

So, the clearest decline in trust is a very local decline—trust in neighbors, trust in the neighborhood—but the result still looks negative (but smaller) at the national level: people who live in diverse neighborhoods tend to think their neighbors are noticeably less trustworthy and probably think their fellow national citizens are less trustworthy too.

These authors look at the same kind of "well-what-abouts" that Putnam did, and the negative result is still there even when you ask, "Well, is it that diverse neighborhoods are poorer? Is it that diverse neighborhoods have higher crime or unemployment rates? Is it that the respondents themselves are less educated?" Those questions matter, but they aren't the whole story. Even knowing quite a lot about the neighborhood and knowing quite a lot about the person being asked, "Can you trust your neighbors?" it's still the case that people are more likely to say they don't trust their neighbors when they're in an ethnically diverse neighborhood.

The message here is clear, nearly unequivocal: when it comes to social trust, greater ethnic diversity is a weakness.

Ethnic Conflict: Alas, All Too Common

By some measures, the most violent riot in American history was a deadly pogrom against Black Americans, the Tulsa Race Massacre of 1921. In Southeast Asia, anti-Chinese riots have been a horrifying staple of the last few centuries, with 1969's "13 May incident" in Malaysia standing out, with probably hundreds dead. And in Europe, the Shoah. These are but a few of the horrifying ethnic slaughters of the last few centuries.

While thinkers from Aristotle to Marx and beyond thought that economic and social class were surely the most important drivers of social conflict, there's another rival for that top spot. As economists Joan Esteban and Debraj Ray put it in 2008 in the *American Economic Review*: "Many, if not most, of the conflicts we observe today are ethnic in nature."[31]

But why are so many conflicts ethnic conflicts? And are ethnic divisions almost unavoidably risky? Another team of economists took a clever approach, one that fuses chapter 1 with this one. Klaus Desmet, Ignacio Ortuño-Ortín, and Romain Wacziarg used "survey data for 76 countries" and found "that ethnic identity is a significant predictor of cultural values."[32] This might sound like they're stating the obvious, but they emphasize a subtle point that's easy to miss: even though ethnic identity predicts cultural values on average, countries with a lot of *diversity in values* aren't more likely to have a lot of *ethnic diversity*, and vice versa. Some countries have a lot of ethnic diversity but not much cultural diversity—citizens broadly agree on the role of family, God, and work even amid lots of ethnic diversity; and some countries have a lot of cultural diversity (think of religious diversity) without having much ethnic diversity. So for the planet as a whole, ethnically diverse countries aren't particularly culturally diverse—or in academic jargon, they aren't particularly culturally *fractionalized*, broken into little pieces.

You might think this is pushing toward a big I-guess-we-really-all-*can*-get-along conclusion, but that's not where Desmet and his coauthors went. They're economists, so they're willing, when necessary, to tell uncomfortable truths. What they find is that even though ethnic diversity and cultural diversity aren't typically paired together, when they are, it's a powder keg:

> However, in countries where ethnicity is more strongly predictive of culture . . . violent conflict is more likely, and public goods provision tends to be lower.[33]

When ethnicity and culture move together, when ethnically diverse groups disagree with each other on cultural issues, the chance of violence rises. The second cost they mention—lower public goods provision—means that there will usually be less spending on things that everyone uses together: roads, public health systems, clean water, trash pickup, things like that. Part of the reason people are willing to support taxes for things they may or may not value is that they have some fellow-feeling for the whole community. But ethnic tension, sadly, dulls that sense of community and shrinks support for government spending on those shared projects.

This link between diversity and public goods spending has been reported many times, in research from around the world. As a team of researchers from Georgetown, UCLA, Columbia, and Stanford studying ethnic diversity within Uganda recently put it: "The empirical connection between ethnic heterogeneity and the underprovision of public goods is widely accepted."[34]

So, does greater ethnic diversity just shrink the size of government? That's what some small-government activists have hoped for—that greater ethnic diversity would reduce the demand for government overall, pushing nations toward smaller and smaller government. It's possible that's part of the picture, but a 2011 summary in the *Journal of Economic Surveys* note some studies reporting that a lot of the spending just shifts from shared goods, like better highways, used by all ethnicities, toward more private goods, like scholarships or government jobs targeted for politically favored ethnic groups.

> Ethnic diversity seems to lead to a shift from public spending on public goods to the public provision of private goods, arguably because the latter can be targeted to particular ethnic groups.[35]

But perhaps more important than whether government dollars are spent on roads or cushy government jobs is whether people feel that they can get along with each other, trust each other, work out conflicts without resorting to violence. The fall in public goods spending in ethnically diverse societies might well be a symptom of a problem—social distrust—more than a problem itself.

Desmet and his coauthors have helped us to see a key reason why ethnic diversity is so often associated with social conflict—because ethnic diversity amplifies the effects of cultural differences. Cultural conflict is risky enough, but when different cultural worldviews match up roughly with different ethnicities, the risk is even greater. We've already seen that cultural differences tend to persist for generations across different ethnic groups in the United States, Canada, and Europe, so the risk of cultural conflict is certainly there. And as in the Dr. Seuss story of the Sneetches—where some birds have stars on their bellies and discriminate against those without—small ethnic differences can easily be both self-reinforcing and a focal point for the cultural outrage of others. So, both real and imagined cultural differences can make ethnic conflict more dangerous, more costly, more deadly than other cultural conflicts. It's a multiplier effect, with risks of downsides all around. The more we dive into the scholarly research on ethnic diversity, the harder it becomes to say that ethnic diversity is usually a strength.

What Does the Doctor Order?

But at least publicly, elites in Western Europe and North America have gone all-in on the theory that our ethnic diversity is our strength—even though the research suggests it's a double-edged sword in the workplace, a nudge toward lower trust in the local neighborhood, and a multiplier of social conflict for the nation. Yes, there are plans and proposals and training programs and social media memes designed to reduce the costs of ethnic diversity, but at this point those treatments are the ivermectin of social science— possibly good, possibly bad, possibly pointless. And if things don't go well, there's no FDA-certified rescue treatment for the costs of ethnic diversity.

What we now know about these costs of ethnic diversity is enough to spur a doctor—the fake kind, one with a Ph.D.—to give some advice: ethnic diversity has some costs, some risks—not overwhelming, but too big to ignore. That means that if a nation is going to choose to increase its ethnic diversity, it should be cautious about doing so unless there's a big, obvious upside to counterbalance those risks. Two important examples:

> Welcoming immigrants who have substantially more education, more job skills, more pro-market attitudes, than the average citizen. If a nation goes down that path, there will be adjustment costs, difficulties, even a risk of greater ethnic violence—but prosperity, human flourishing is worth sacrificing for. This is the story told in the preface.

> Welcoming refugees who've suffered great violence in their homelands (possibly due to their home country's own ethnic conflict). Being humane is costly, and is often truly risky. But being humane makes us better at being human, and that is a big, obvious upside.

East Asia's economic successes—Japan, South Korea, maybe throw in China—have followed a low-diversity, low-immigration policy. And among the rich nations, quite a few have taken the high-skilled, high-ethnic-diversity approach—including Singapore, the former nation of Hong Kong (RIP), Australia, New Zealand, and Canada. Over the next few decades, we'll see how those two approaches turn out compared to each other. But far more importantly, we'll be able to compare those countries to other rich countries—like the U.S., France, Italy, and the UK—that have apparently built their immigration policies around the outdated, unscientific cliché that our ethnic diversity, in and of itself, is our strength.

4. France   5 percent

5. South Korea   4 percent[3]

Another way to see the big story: the U.S., at 28 percent, and the
entire European Union, at 29 percent, together create over half
the world's total of triadic patents—and with Japan, you're at 88
percent.

Patents are just one way to look at innovative activity. Another
is a nation's total spending on research and development of new
ideas, new methods, new products. These measures have their own
flaws—some countries will have tax rules that encourage firms to
inflate the R & D numbers in order to qualify for tax credits, for
instance. But as you'll see these different measures of innovative
activity—patents, R & D spending, and later the total number of
publications in science journals—all end up telling much the same
story. And when very different methods tell us nearly the same
story, that's a sign we're on the right track. Here are the world's
top five R & D spenders in 2009—in total dollars, not dollars per
person:[4]

1. U.S. $370 billion

2. Japan $140 billion

3. China $110 billion

4. Germany $70 billion

5. South Korea $40 billion

Total R & D spending that year in the OECD—a rich- and
middle-income country club of thirty-eight countries—was $900
billion, and adding in China makes it about a trillion. Since almost
all R & D occurs either in the OECD or in China, that means that
the U.S. and Japan make up about half the world's total R & D,
and the world's top five make up over two-thirds of the world total.
FYI: France and the U.K. are just behind Korea, and Taiwan is
also a big player in R & D. So far, it looks the world's biggest idea-
makers are quite likely to have high Ts in their nation's SAT scores.

And a final measure of scientifically valuable new ideas: the top five countries with the most publications in leading scholarly science journals in 2018, according to Nature Index, are the following:[5]

1. U.S.

2. China

3. Germany

4. U.K.

5. Japan

These nations—on all these top-five lists—are rare, idea-generating treasures that we all should value whether we live in one of them or not. So, what makes these idea-creating countries different from the rest? All the countries on these top-five lists—triadic patents, R & D spending, and scientific publications—have at least two important traits in common.

First, they all have fairly large populations. South Korea is the smallest at 52 million; the U.K. and France are each just under 70 million. China and the U.S. are by far the largest, with 1.4 billion and 330 million respectively. By contrast, the median country on the planet has a population of about 9 million, and even if we chose to omit the dozens of countries with populations of under a million, the median country would still only have about 11 million souls.

Second, these high-innovation countries all have high migration-adjusted T scores, high Year 1500 scores in Comin, Easterly, and Gong's Tech History index. (Of course, without the migration adjustment, the U.S.'s Tech History score would be quite low, but the others would be little changed. The T scores for most nations have been little-changed by migration.)

Of the two, the T level is the stronger predictor of innovation. Of the world's ten most populous nations, only China and the U.S. show up on any of the above high-innovation lists, while the rest of the top ten—

India (1.4 billion),

Indonesia (270 million),

Pakistan (220 million),

Brazil (210 million),

Nigeria (200 million),

Bangladesh (160 million),

Russia (150 million),

Mexico (130 million)

—show up nowhere near the top of these high-innovation lists, although Brazil and Russia deserve honorable mentions, bronze medals in the global innovation Olympics. So, most of the world's valuable ideas are coming from places with lots of people and lots of ancestral experience with good technology.

It's an amazing fact: there are almost two hundred countries in the world, and yet around half a dozen of them are inventing the vast majority of the world's valuable new ideas in science and technology. It's little surprise that all of these high innovators are countries with bigger populations than most: if great scientists are literally one in a million, then every extra million citizens means one more great scientist whose ideas can shape the entire world— and a nation of a hundred million people will have a hundred times more great ideas than a million-person country. This fact shows up in lists of Nobel laureates per country: the Nobel-laureates-per-capita list looks quite different from the total-Nobel-laureates list.

Let's look at just the science Nobels (where, yes, I'll include economics):

Total Nobel science laureates	Nobel laureates per capita
1. United States (350)	1. Saint Lucia (pop. 180,000, 1 winner)
2. United Kingdom (109)	2. Luxembourg (pop. 590,000, 2 winners)
3. Germany (93)	3. Switzerland
4. France (39)	4. Austria
5. Switzerland (25)	5. Denmark

And Japan would be number 6 in the left column with 24 Nobels. Switzerland, with just 9 million people, shows up on both lists—the world owes the Swiss a debt. But as a rule, it's hard to be a top creator of world-shaking ideas if you don't have a big population. If you want to find a lot of gold, get a lot of people panning for gold.

But how can the T index (Tech History in 1500) matter? Well, there's the obvious story that the more things change, the more they stay the same, so if your nation's ancestors tended to be comfortable with tech in 1500, your nation has a good chance of tech success today. But that's not really capturing the why; it doesn't explain the links the chain of cause and effect running from past to present.

As economist James Ang already showed us in chapter 4, Tech History is a powerful predictor of the quality of a nation's institutions, its governance. With the exception of China, all the top idea-creating nations do well on all the institutional quality lists—low corruption, a wide embrace of markets, a decent legal system. And notice that China, although in only the middle of global rankings on typical institutional quality measures, does have scale, a massive population, going for it—about four times that of the United States and sixty times that of South Korea. But even then, China is a bit uneven on idea creation.

So, while on a per-capita basis, China still makes the top 25 percent in global R & D spending, even in total numbers, China never did well on triadic patents at all. When it comes to big global, marketable ideas, institutional quality is almost surely holding China back, way back, and it's making up for it with quantity. China has moved up a lot in government quality over the past three decades, but it's got a long way to go before it catches up to the world's other majority-Chinese countries: Taiwan and Singapore, and in a limited sense, Macau and Hong Kong.

But let's not just assume that good government institutions drive innovation. Let's try to, well, not exactly prove it like a mathematical theorem, but let's at least look to see if there's real-world evidence that good governance helps generate good ideas. We've already seen that the Deep Roots scores—SAT and the rest—capture traits that can cause changes in government quality over the very long run, and we've already seen that politically important attitudes substantially migrate and last for generations, almost surely shaping government policy. What we should look for now is whether changes in government institutions, changes in the rules of the game, matter for innovation, for R & D, and for patents.

And here, the evidence is abundant. In 2013, two economists, Edinaldo Tebaldi of Bryant University and Bruce Elmslie of the University of New Hampshire, ran some simple, clean tests that create a great first look at the question.[6] They start off answering the simplest question: do countries with stronger institutions have more patents? They use three measures, two of which we've already run across and which were created by the World Bank: a Rule of Law measure ("the extent to which agents have confidence in and abide by the rules of society . . . as well as the likelihood of crime and violence"[7]) and a blend of indices they call an Institutional Quality Index. The third measure is a Risk of Expropriation measure (the chance the government or someone with good government connections will take your stuff), created by a private organization, Political Risk Services. They also use two measures of patents: the U.S. Patent and Trademark Office index (if you've got a big idea, you usually want to patent it in the U.S. so that Americans can't immediately copy it) and World Bank measure of patents "granted by each country's patent office to its residents," a truly global measure. I'll focus on the U.S. measure, though both tell nearly the same story. As the authors emphasize, the U.S. measure counts only the number of patents granted to nonresidents—that is, inventions created in countries other than the U.S. whose inventors wish to patent their ideas in the U.S. market.[8]

The relationship between the institutional quality measures and total (not per person) patent counts is about as strong the relationship between, for example, height and weight among young adult men: taller men usually weigh more than shorter men, but there are some big exceptions. By normal standards, that's a pretty strong relationship; institutional differences across countries predict around 70 percent of the differences in U.S.-filed patent counts across countries.[9]

So, better institutions predict more patents—no surprise, given what we've seen in the rankings so far. But Tebaldi and Elmslie go further and ask whether maybe that relationship just happens because countries with good institutions have more researchers or publish more books; maybe the institutional quality is "nice" but not really important. They run a lot of statistical tests to check that theory out, and every single time, the good-institutions-are-nice-but-not-important theory fails the test. It turns out that institutions matter—and they matter a lot for predicting high levels of patents. Even if you know many other things about a country—the number of researchers, the number of books written there, how far the country is from the sea coast, the average temperature, how densely populated the country's adults are—the institutional measures all still matter. And the predicted changes are massive: a move from the bottom of the government quality indexes to the top predicts about a hundred-fold increase in the number of patents per year. And every one-unit change on the five-point World Bank institutional quality scale predicts a bit more than a five-fold boost in patents.

These numbers sound too big to believe at first, but they're reminders that there's almost no patenting, and almost no formal R & D, going on in most of the world's countries. Around fifty countries file zero patents with the U.S. government in the average year—but German organizations yearly file around 18,000 patents in the U.S. These gaps in patenting are much, much bigger than the already massive gaps in income per person of twenty times to thirty times between the poor and rich nations. And while the U.S. is spending over a third of a trillion dollars each year on R & D, most countries are spending so little that it's not even worth measuring.

Dozens of countries measure their R & D at a few million dollars per year, about one-hundred thousandth of the U.S. level. That's pretty close to an infinite difference.

But while these one-time cross-country comparisons are interesting and a very good first step, they're not even close to a true experiment. Tebaldi and Elmslie checked to see if coastlines or books could beat out government quality as a predictor of patent, but you're still ultimately comparing one country to another, where what you'd hope to do is to compare the country to itself, while just changing one element of that country—the quality of its government—and then checking to see how that predicts changes in that nation's innovation. That approach would bring us closer to a true controlled scientific experiment.

Fortunately, economists have a classic way to come closer to that comparison: look at the very same country at different points in time, and check what happens to innovative activity after measured government quality changes. Case studies are one version of this. For example, how did Chinese innovation change when the country grew more market-friendly from the 1980s onward? (Spoiler: China started patenting a lot more and did a lot more R & D.) But it's easy to run that same kind of compare-the-country-to-itself test simultaneously for the entire planet at once. We call that a "fixed effect panel regression," (don't worry, that term won't be on the final exam), and economist Cong Wang of Australia's Monash University ran just such a test in 2013.[10]

Wang first ran pretty much the same tests as Tebaldi and Elmslie. He checked to see if the World Bank governance indicators can help predict a nation's level of R & D and of patenting per person, and indeed they do, even if you know quite few other facts about a country. These are just the usual one-slice-in-time, cross-country comparisons—but he ran more and different tests than in the other paper. For instance, he tests out more than one measure of institutional quality. He tries the World Bank measures we've seen before, the International Country Risk Guide (ICRG) measures (a private-sector index of government quality sometimes used to assess whether a nation is likely to pay off its debts), and the widely used Polity measure of democracy, which is in part a measure of whether the government mostly acts under the impersonal rule of law rather than under the rule of a personal leader unbeholden to the law. And any way Wang runs it, institutional quality is a good predictor of innovation. Elmslie and Tebaldi's results weren't a fluke, and now we know that similar results hold for R & D spending and not just for patents.

But then Wang moves to the new test: What if you compare the country to itself? What if you use a fixed effect panel regression to give the computer the option, a real option, of telling you something like this:

> Actually, when one country's government quality rises for a few years or falls for a few years, that doesn't predict any change over time at all in R & D or in patents. Short-term and medium-term changes in these government quality indexes don't predict anything important out there in the real world, certainly not R & D spending. Quit getting so worked up over these year-to-year or decade-to-decade wiggles in these government quality indices!

Wang offers his computer the opportunity to tell him just that. And when Wang goes on to these stronger tests, these "fixed effect panel" tests that compare each country to itself as its institutional quality changes over the years, increases in government quality still predict increases in innovation.

He also checks that the result isn't driven by other factors that are changing over the years, factors that include the country's openness to trade, its level of financial sophistication, and its level of education. So even knowing those things about a country, government quality still predicts R & D intensity. The relationship between institutions and R & D, while strong, becomes weaker in the other tests. But then again, Wang is looking at the relationship between this year's government quality and this year's R & D intensity. It's pretty likely that this year's R & D intensity depends on both the past and the likely future path of government quality: businesses making big R & D investments care about years of stability and good governance; they care about persistence. And in some other tests that Wang runs, he indeed finds evidence that the long-run effect of institutions on R & D is bigger than the one-year effect.

And repeatedly Wang shows that his results hold up across multiple measures of R & D intensity and multiple measures of institutional quality. He checks to see how changes in institutional quality predict changes in

the percentage of scientists and engineers involved in R & D as a percentage of the nation's total labor force,

R&D spending as a percentage of the overall economy, and

total patents divided by the nation's total labor force.

This isn't a case where one statistic tells one story and another statistic tells another. Wang's results, together with Tebaldi and Elmslie's, make a strong case that government quality itself causes higher levels of innovation. That means that China's combination of high innovation with mediocre institutional quality is a rare exception to the rule—it's the national equivalent of the person who didn't wear his seatbelt but still walked away from the horrific crash. The wise don't build their policy choices around exceptions to the rule; they build their policy choices around the rule.

Wang sums up his findings—and takes the author's prerogative of saying that yes, he really is documenting causation, not just correlation or prediction:

First, institutions have a direct effect on R & D; this relationship is robust after we [account] for the effects of religion, legal origin, geography, human capital, openness to trade and financial development on R & D. Various types of political institutions quality as measured by the ICRG, [World Bank] and Polity all showed strong influence [of institutions] on R & D expenditure, personnel and output (patents).[11]

The relationship running from good government to high innovation—true on average, not in every case—looks pretty well nailed down. So, when a nation changes in ways that hurt its government quality, that probably hurts its innovation down the road. Now it's time to see how high innovation boosts productivity and incomes—not just in the country where the ideas are invented, but the whole world round. It's time to see how innovation in one country is the world's gain.

The Magic of Diffusion

Research performed abroad is about two-thirds as potent as domestic research. Together the United States and Japan drive at least two-thirds of the growth of each of the countries in our sample.

—Jonathan Eaton and Samuel Kortum, *International Economic Review*, 1999[12]

Back in the late 1990s, two economists at Boston University—Jonathan Eaton and Samuel Kortum—tried to see how quickly and how thoroughly new high-tech concepts and practices spread from one country to another, and then they tried to see how those new ideas grow the economy of the nation that started using those new ideas. Their big conclusion is in the quote just above. So, we're starting with one answer—an influential, well-cited answer—to the question, How much does high-tech research in one country shape the economies of other countries? Let's check out some of the tools they used to reach that conclusion, and then let's see how their view has held up over the decades.

One method they used: surveys of actual businesses. They reported the results of an influential 1980 study by economists Edwin Mansfield of the University of Pennsylvania (Ben Franklin's school) and Anthony Romeo of the University of Connecticut.[13] They interviewed top executives at U.S.-based multinational corporations—companies with headquarters in the U.S. but with branches in multiple countries—and asked them a question a bit like this: "Once you figure out that a new technology works well in your U.S. branch, how long does it usually take to spread that technology to your firm's international branches located in rich countries?"

They interviewed thirty-one manufacturing firms, twenty-six of them among the five hundred largest in the U.S. The twenty-six were chosen "essentially at random" and included "a wide variety of industries, including chemicals, drugs, petroleum, electrical equipment and electronics, machinery, instruments, glass, food, and rubber." [14]

And they didn't just run interviews, taking the word of the executives as gospel: "the firm's internal records were used to determine the year when each technology was first introduced in the United States."[15]

What was the average age of an idea before it spread to the subsidiary? About six years. That's a long time for a good idea to spread just to a foreign branch of your own company! And that was how long it took when the foreign branch was in a rich country; the same corporate leaders said that when the foreign branch was in a developing country, it took an average of ten years. That may well have sped up by now, but even then, that was a long time to leave a good idea on the table, using it only in one branch of a big company. It's one sign that change is hard, even when the change is clearly an improvement. And if it takes an average of six years for ideas to move within the same company, it surely takes even longer for good ideas to fully disseminate between firms. The same survey shows that even when two separate corporations make plans to share ideas via licensing or joint ventures, it takes an average of thirteen years before the ideas get passed from one firm to another. That's half a generation.

Mansfield and Romeo went even further by asking seventy big British firms how quickly and how often they adopted technology invented by U.S. firms. Twenty percent of the UK firms said new

U.S. tech was an important source of new ideas—quite a lot when you consider that the U.S. is just one of the world's most innovative economies. The percentage was "higher in the electrical equipment (including electronics and computers) and general engineering industries than in the others."[16] The best ideas get borrowed a lot.

What's Important?

A sidenote: you might rightly wonder how these British firms decide whether a new technology invented in the U.S. is "important" to them. Mansfield and Romeo wondered the same thing. They didn't want to force a definition on the people responding to the interviews and surveys, so they left the question open-ended. But then they followed up and learned something quite fascinating about decision-making in big businesses. They bury a big story in a footnote:

> Initially the firms were permitted to use whatever definition of "important" that they regarded as appropriate. Then they were asked to specify what they meant by this term. Based on the replies, it appears that they generally regarded any benefit that enhanced profits by 1 percent or more as important. . . . There is no evidence of substantial differences among firms in the definition used.[17]

Consider the biggest UK manufacturer today, Unilever, which owns many well-known brands including Lipton, Dove, and Hellman's. In 2019, its profits (i.e., its net income) were €6 billion. So, anything that would boost profits by €60 million a year would be important, and anything much less than that would be . . . well, it would be impolite to say "unimportant," but when time and management attention are in short supply, it's something Unilever will probably let slide by.

How Good Ideas Spread—Eventually

Mansfield and Romeo also asked U.S. corporations how long they thought their foreign competitors took to figure out the U.S. technologies well enough to create competing products. They gave a variety of answers—from less than six months to over six years—

but the average answer was four years. The American executives thought the foreign competitors used a variety of methods to get the information they needed:

> The most frequent channel by which the technology "leaked out" was reverse engineering. . . . That is, non-U.S. competitors took apart and analyzed the new or modified product to gain insights into the relevant technology. Also, information provided by patents was judged to play a significant role; and non-U.S. firms sometimes gained access to the technology by hiring away personnel [from a U.S. firm with valuable tech].[18]

Taking machines apart, reading patents, hiring experts—there's more than one way for great ideas to diffuse to other countries. Industrial espionage is part of the story as well, in ways large and small. For instance, in the classic journalistic tale of 1970s computer innovation mentioned in chapter 5, *The Soul of a New Machine*, Tracy Kidder said that a computer engineer at one small firm used some connections to secretly visit a company that had bought its competitor's minicomputer—and on the secret visit the engineer spent hours looking inside the soul of the competitor's product for design inspiration.[19]

It's clear that learning how to imitate, emulate, and build upon great high-tech ideas is hard work—it usually takes years of effort. While I started off the chapter glibly saying that it's free to copy music lyrics or even the theory of gravity, in real life copying is expensive. Partly that's because companies with great ideas usually try to keep other firms from using those ideas—through patents, trade secrets, and nondisclosure agreements, for example—but partly it's just because imitation is extremely difficult. Most NBA players would gladly become as good as LeBron James if they could, but none can—and that's a case where everyone can watch exactly what James does on the basketball court—in replay, in slow motion—and where the majority of his key competitors—other NBA players—have actually played against him!

Athletic imitation, artistic imitation, musical imitation, even imitation of great wines—in all these cases, there are enormous amounts of money to be made, fame to be earned, if people can imitate the most famous in the field, if the also-rans can act at least sort of like the best in the world. And yet those potential imitators rarely, rarely succeed in their attempts—the best might get 10 percent of the way there, 30 percent of the way there and might make small fortunes for themselves, but even those successes are rare. And if successful imitation is rare when the final product is perceptible to the eye, ear, nose, and mouth, what hope is there for imitating business processes, good corporate cultures, or just the right way to make the smartphone battery so it lasts eight hours rather than six?

Consider generic drugs. Economists Michele Boldrin and Michael Levine of Washington University of St. Louis note that back in the 1990s, when India's government allowed pharmaceutical companies to copy any drug in the world, it still took the typical Indian pharmaceutical firm four years to come up with a useful copy of the original drug.[20] And that's for drugs that are already patented elsewhere—and since a patent requires a complete chemical description of the drug, that means it takes these firms years to copy a recipe that's already sitting in front of them.

Slow Spread: Creating Ideas We All (Eventually) Enjoy

The evidence on the slow spread of great ideas from one firm to another is ground level, based on surveys and interviews and case studies, and they all tell the same story: a slow diffusion of valuable ideas from one country to another. Both *slow* and *spread* are important here, and each captures part of Paul Romer's message about innovation: the "spread" reminds us that good ideas eventually get imitated, and so are valuable the world over. The "slow" is a big part of the reason the ideas get invented in the first place. If competitors copied good ideas immediately, then there wouldn't be much incentive to invent.

The slow spread means than an inventor can usually make some money before the copiers make the invention cheap and widely available. Apple had its mouse-driven graphical user interface in the Lisa in 1983 and the Macintosh in 1984, and while Microsoft offered a crude Windows 1.0 in 1985, Windows wasn't a hit until version 3.0 arrived in 1990. Apple surely suspected it would have the market to itself for a while, at least long enough to justify the big R & D effort that led to the mass-market success of the Mac. Patented drugs eventually become generics; American cars eventually become as reliable as Japanese cars from twenty years earlier. Stewart Brand was right when he said, "Information wants to be free," but the Rolling Stones were also right: "You can't always get what you want." And the time between the invention of an idea and the idea becoming common knowledge (at least to experts) creates the innovation incentive.

The Quants Measure Diffusion

Bronwyn Hall, professor emerita of economics at the University of California, Berkeley, has long been a leader in the study of both the causes and the effects of R & D. In 2010, she coauthored a survey essay that looked back on decades of work by herself and others on just how R & D in one firm spills over to other firms, other industries, and other countries. She sums up the size of these beneficial spillovers of R & D: "In general they have been found to be quite large, but rather imprecisely estimated."[21]

That's often the case in real-world economics: lots of noisy estimates, as fuzzy as old telescope images of the planet Jupiter. Hall cites a classic 1995 paper by the IMF's David Coe and Harvard's Elhanan Helpman. It used the best data of the time: R & D spending from the G-7 countries, a group of high-population, high-productivity countries (Canada, the U.S., Italy, Japan, Germany, France, and the UK). Hall sums up their finding: roughly a quarter of the benefits from R & D in G-7 countries accrues to their trading partners.[22]

So again, productive ideas spread to other countries. It's a famous paper, so it's been beaten up a lot over the decades, with a lot of different theoretical and statistical critiques. Some studies find bigger international spillovers—like the "two-thirds as potent" result from

Eaton and Kortum noted above—and some find a smaller or maybe even a zero effect. But Hall looks at many results and brings some good economic thinking to bear in her conclusion. In countries that spend very little on R & D, she concludes that businesses probably take advantage of the work of others: it is likely that small R & D spenders have relatively more to gain from foreign R & D by the sheer size of the absorbable knowledge.[23]

So Denmark, with a population of 5 million, probably uses many more ideas from Germany (population 83 million) than the other way around. The small, in this way exploit the large—another reminder that every nation relies on the inventions mostly created in just a few nations.

Protecting and Improving the I-7

The entire world stands to gain when the biggest countries with the best institutions innovate. And we all stand to lose when they don't. That means the entire world has a stake in the governance, the institutional quality, of the world's seven most innovative nations:

China
France
Germany
Japan
South Korea
United Kingdom
United States

And since SAT scores, transplanted cultural traits, and some forms of diversity appear to shape a nation's institutional quality, that means that the entire world has a stake in the SAT scores, transplanted cultural traits, and forms of diversity that exist in these seven high-innovation nations, our world's I-7. If any of these nations takes even a small hit to the quality of its government, within a decade or two that probably means a big hit to the world's stock of great new ideas. And there aren't any heavily populated, well-governed, strong Tech History nations waiting in the wings to take up the slack if an I-7 nation drifts toward mediocrity. Outside of China and the U.S., the world's high-population nations lack great prospects for South Korean, Japanese, or German levels of innovation. It's as if we're ninety minutes into the movie, and the I-7 are the only heroes left standing who can battle the supervillain of scientific sluggishness.

Citizens of every country on earth should be more than just "concerned" about improving governance in these seven nations. Since these seven nations create the vast majority of the world's innovation, this calls for more than mere concern. Instead, it calls for obsession.

7 The Chinese Diaspora: Building the Capitalist Road

The Chinese diaspora has . . . certain unique cultural characteristics that potentially could be conducive to economic growth.

—Jan Priebe and Robert Rudolf, *World Development*, 2015[1]

UNLIKE EUROPE, CHINA NEVER HAD A dark age; it never had a centuries-long slump in population, lifespan, prosperity, and culture. China did have one terrible century, though. It lasted from the last decades of the Qing dynasty in the late 1800s through the horrors of civil war and Japanese invasion, through the self-inflicted starvation of the Great Leap Forward and the chaos of the Cultural Revolution. The latest wave of China's great suffering was spearheaded by China's Communist dictator Mao Zedong. Mao spent much of his energy fighting enemies within whom he called "capitalist roaders" (走資派), people who pretended outwardly to be great Communists but who were secretly pushing, one way or another, for market competition, free enterprise, and an economic system with a strong focus on profit and loss and efficiency.

Many thought that Mao was paranoid, looking for capitalists under the bed, seeing market-driven bogeymen in his dreams and in his nightmares. Of course, of course, no true-hearted member of the Communist Party's inner circle could be a secret capitalist—the very idea was laughable! Of course, the revolution was made up of true believers!

In the 1970s, during Mao's last years, the Communist Party named and shamed one of the greatest of these alleged capitalist roaders. Indeed, he was named the "Number Two Capitalist Roader," and party leaders said he was covertly undermining the glorious destiny of "Communism with Chinese Characteristics." Obviously, this was pure paranoia all around. Imitating Senator Joe McCarthy's critics, one might have said to those making such an outrageous accusation, "At long last, have you left no sense of decency?"

And then Mao died, and within a few years a new leader took power, and that new leader took China rapidly if incompletely right down that capitalist road. You already know who that leader is: China's Number Two Capitalist Roader, Deng Xiaoping.

Two lessons:

1. Just because you're paranoid doesn't mean you're wrong.

2. Even the horrifying oppression of Communist dictatorship couldn't keep China away from its capitalist destiny.

And as we've already seen, outside China, every country with a majority that's of Chinese descent is strongly capitalist, strongly market oriented, and prosperous: Taiwan, Singapore, tiny Macau, and Hong Kong (even if Hong Kong is, alas, not much of a separate country any longer). China is, by far, the world's poorest majority-Chinese country—though it's catching up at an astonishing pace. It apparently takes a while to shake off the big mistake of Communism. It's too bad the other side, eventually driven to Taiwan, didn't win China's civil war. If the Nationalists had won, China wouldn't have wasted decades on its big mistake; it almost surely would have become market friendly much sooner, and over a billion people would be far richer, healthier, more comfortable today.

Taiwan, Singapore, Macau, Hong Kong—those four Chinese-majority countries appear to be grafting China's Deep Roots of prosperity, China's high SAT scores from 1500, China's legacy of good governance and competent bureaucracy, and China's legacy of Confucian culture onto multiple lands. Chinese migrants bring the heritage of the Ming Dynasty to lands beyond the reach of the great Ming emperors—Singapore is 1,600 miles away, Ming-era Taiwan spent a portion of the era as a Dutch colony, and Hong Kong and Macau were lightly populated fishing villages now mostly populated by the descendants of emigrants and refugees from mainland China. China's great heritage has migrated to these lands with the Chinese migrants.

These four neo-Chinas (a term we can use in parallel with the "neo-Europes" that include North America and Australasia) are now among the richest in the world. All are among the top 10 percent of richest countries per person; all have higher average incomes per person than Australia or Canada or France. And none have natural resources to thank for their prosperity. Their best geographic feature is excellent access to the ocean; all but Hong Kong are island countries, and Hong Kong is mostly but not completely a collection of islands. But all four also have geographic features hurting them as well. Singapore is essentially on the equator, and the rest are pretty close. Taiwan, the northernmost of the four, is at the same 25 degrees latitude as Key West, Florida; Riyadh, Saudi Arabia; and the small oasis town of Guelta Zemmur in the territory of Western Sahara.

You've already seen that countries closer to the equator tend to be poorer, even if we're not sure why—but the punishing heat and humidity close to the equator aren't holding these four majority-Chinese nations back. So, geography is, for them, pretty much a wash. None are close to landlocked, but all are in the heat zone. Geographic theories of national prosperity are popular, but they're not up to the task of explaining the prosperity of China's offshoots.

But cultural transplant theory is up to the task—and not just in these four offshoots. For centuries, emigrants from China moved to every country in Southeast Asia, and wherever they went in sizable but not overwhelming numbers, Chinese immigrants became what Yale's Amy Chua properly named "market dominant minorities."[2] Thailand, Malaysia, Indonesia, the Philippines—people from China moved to all these nations, usually thinking they'd move back. But they often ended up staying, though typically keeping up some degree of Chinese cultural practices and retaining the Chinese language. Indeed, a standard practice in most of these countries and in academic research is still to refer to descendants of Chinese migrants as "Chinese immigrants," even if their ancestors arrived from China centuries ago. And on average, first-, second-, and third-generation Chinese immigrants wound up much richer, more prosperous, and better educated than the indigenous populations in the countries they moved to.

Why were Chinese immigrants so much more successful? Hong Kong-based writer Lynn Pan drove home the cultural persistence theory in her fascinating, well-reviewed book *Sons of the Yellow Emperor: A History of the Chinese Diaspora*. She notes:

> The empire from which [these Chinese immigrants] originated antedated the Southeast Asian societies in civilization and commercial development and greatly exceeded them in wealth and sophistication.[3]

And to a substantial degree, those Chinese migrants carried the Deep Roots of Chinese excellence with them to their new homes. In this chapter, I'm going to show that the case study approach—one that focuses on countries in Southeast Asia—will tell the same story as the statistical approaches economists love. When it comes to economic prosperity in Southeast Asia, the more things change, the more they stay the same—as long as you adjust for migration.

Southeast Asia's Glorious Chinese Diaspora

As China's Qing Dynasty declined in the 1800s, Chinese migrants moved to many countries where they both started and ended as ethnic minorities. Four in particular deserve our attention: Malaysia, Thailand, Indonesia, and the Philippines. For all four, I'm reporting in table 7.1 the Putterman-Weil estimate of percent *net* Chinese immigration since 1500. For comparison, I also report another widely used estimate[4] of the percent of the population that was of Chinese descent in 1990, as well as 2019 income per person.

The Putterman-Weil estimates differ somewhat from the other Chinese ethnicity estimates—ethnicity is fluid, to a great degree subjective, so no surprise. And the Putterman-Weil Philippines estimate, in particular, is zero because there were already quite a few Chinese traders in the Philippines before 1500. But both net Chinese migration and current Chinese population yield the same rank order.

And notice: the rank order between the Chinese share of the population and income per person is, at least for these four heavily studied countries, a perfect relationship. More Chinese immigrants in the past, more prosperity today. Even if I included more Southeast Asian countries beyond these four—we'll come to them later—that relationship holds up quite well overall though it's no longer a perfectly matched ranking. No matter how we look at it, across Southeast Asia, there's a strong relationship between the Chinese share of the population and current prosperity—especially when we note that majority-Chinese Taiwan, Hong Kong, Macau, and Singapore each have incomes per person of at least $55,000 per year.

Earlier chapters, especially chapter 1, have already given us good

TABLE 7.1. Two leading measures of Chinese ancestry in Southeast Asia and 2019 income per person.

	Net Chinese immigration since 1500 (P/W)	Population of Chinese descent, 1980 (Rauch)	Income per person, 2019
Malaysia	25%	33%	$30,000
Thailand	14%	10%	$19,000
Indonesia	2%	4%	$12,000
Philippines	0%	2%	$9,000

Sources: Putterman and Weil (2010); Rauch and Trindade (2002).

reasons to think that a lot of this relationship is truly cause and effect—that people bring key cultural traits from their home countries to their new countries, that a lot of those traits persist for generations, shaping businesses and governments, and that the migration-adjusted past is prologue. A glance at a map can do even more. It reminds us that great geography can't explain why Malaysia is more productive than Thailand, which is more productive than Indonesia, which is more productive than the Philippines. As far as geography goes, they've all been dealt quite similar hands, pretty close to the equator and with good access to the ocean. Indeed, Manila Bay in the Philippines is among the best natural harbors in the region—arguably the best! And yet the Philippines is the poorest country in this group.

The Maybes of Colonization

But we should kick the tires first before drawing a conclusion: What if today's prosperity was driven by who colonized them? It's worth looking at. The Philippines was a Spanish colony for centuries until the U.S. took over around 1900, and former Spanish colonies have tended to have weaker economies than other similar countries. Thailand always remained nominally and mostly really independent, so we'll set it aside. Indonesia was a Dutch colony, and Malaysia passed from being a Portuguese to a Dutch to a British colony. The Dutch had too few colonies to generalize, but there's at least some evidence that, based on patterns around the world, being a British colony was a net economic plus.

So perhaps we can attribute the Malaysia-Indonesia-Philippines rank order to who colonized them, and who perhaps left some kind of legacy, who planted some kind of Deep Roots of economic success or failure. Maybe it was the colonizer's particular bureaucratic culture, its attitudes toward markets or corruption, its emphasis on childhood education that lasted through the centuries. It's worth a thought, even though the other countries we'll look at in the region will weaken this simple story. Ultimately, the most important part of that colonial legacy may be that some colonizers were better at attracting Chinese immigrants who decided to come and to stay and to massively change the economies to which they migrated.

Non-Economists on the Diaspora

Scholarly histories of Southeast Asia have to wrestle with the big economic role that an often small number of Chinese migrants and their descendants have played in the region. The twelfth edition of Dr. Milton Osborne's leading college textbook, *A History of Southeast Asia*, reports:

> The situation throughout Southeast Asia had a broadly uniform character. . . . Small immigrant communities engaged in commerce that was, for the most part, shunned by Southeast Asians themselves. Of these immigrant communities the Chinese were by far the most important.[5]

This commercial excellence showed up just about everywhere, and it was massive. Paul J. Bolt, a political scientist at the U.S. Air Force Academy writes:

> Before 1942, the overseas Chinese reportedly owned 80 percent to 90 percent of the rice mills in Thailand. Before 1932, they controlled 70 percent to 80 percent of the retail trade in the Philippines, and in 1948 held over 20 percent of commercial assets there. . . . The *Economist* [stated] that as of late 1995 . . . Chinese control two-thirds of the region's retail trade.[6]

And Henry Wai-chung Yeung of the National University of Singapore notes the extremely long-run nature of the economic success of Chinese migrants:

> Over several centuries . . . an informal array of Chinese entrepreneurs, traders, financiers and their closely knit networks of family members and friends came to dominate the economic sphere of the very host countries they later considered "home."[7]

Table 7.2, with data from Bolt's *China and Southeast Asia's Ethnic Chinese*, shows that Chua's expression "market-dominant minority" is no understatement. You can see that in Malaysia, which is around one-third Chinese, firms in the private sector are mostly owned by Chinese immigrants, though the ownership share isn't as high as you might expect. One policy that tends to hold down those numbers is the Malaysian government's systemic program of economic affirmative action for indigenous groups in Malaysia. One study from the 1990s explains how extensive the program was at the time:

> [The Malaysia National Economic Policy] provided incentives and assistance for Malay entry into industrial and commercial endeavours through provision of equity, capital, loan financing, education and training. It aimed to increase Bumiputera [a controversial term referring to ethnic Malays and other indigenous groups] corporate wealth from 2.4% in 1970 to 30% in 1990.[8]

The government didn't reach the 30-percent goal but did manage to increase ethnic Malay wealth to about 20 percent of the corporate sector, in part due to "a growth of state trusts, sheltering the interests of Bumiputera, in the mining and service sectors."[9]

Malaysia thus has a variety of massive affirmative action programs that still exist in various forms in both the private and public

TABLE 7.2. Business success among ethnic Chinese citizens of Southeast Asian countries.

	Population of Chinese descent, 1980	Share of GDP generated by Chinese-immigrant-owned businesses	Share of publicly traded companies owned by Chinese immigrants
Malaysia	33%	60%	61%
Thailand	10%	50%	81%
Indonesia	4%	50%	73%
Philippines	2%	40%	50%

Sources: Rauch and Trindade (2002); Bolt (2000).

sectors. For example, the U.S. State Department noted in a 2018 essay on the investment climate in Malaysia that

> some contacts at U.S. companies have reported that the government monitors the ethnic balance among employees and enforces an ethnic quota system for hiring in certain areas. Race-based preferences in hiring and promotion are widespread in government, government-owned universities and government-linked corporations.[10]

These kinds of programs have had had big payoffs for ethnic Malays and other indigenous groups—a reminder that without these programs, the Chinese role in Malaysia's economy would be even larger.

And it's not just vague "commercial success" that sets Chinese immigrants apart across Southeast Asia. It's also, according to numerous reports, a matter of frugality. Lynn Pan again:

> One loses count of the number of times the overseas Chinese's extreme thrift, their other hallmark, prompted comment, and it is true they were great ones for deferred gratification. . . . They were great savers.[11]

This fact shows up at the cross-country level: China's high savings rate has long prompted discussion, and Singapore, Taiwan, and Hong Kong all have higher-than-average savings rates. But it also shows up when we study immigrants. The study in chapter 1 of savings practices among immigrants in the UK found that third-generation Chinese immigrants tended to save quite a lot compared to immigrants from other countries. While surely there are many exceptions, it is clear that on average, Chinese immigrants across Southeast Asia have been both disproportionate savers and disproportionate builders of the private sectors, regardless of which nation they were living in.

Chinese Immigrants: Bearing the Costs of Ethnic Diversity
The economic success of Chinese immigrants plus the repeated human sin of envy have together fostered centuries of Sinophobia, anti-Chinese sentiment and persecution. Of course, success

itself isn't the only important factor behind the Sinophobia; ethnic conflict is a human perennial, as we've seen. But economic success drives envy of economic success around the world, so Southeast Asia should be no exception to this universal human rule.

Malaysia and Indonesia are the countries where the masses themselves have been most hostile to Chinese immigrants, and both nations have had deadly anti-Chinese riots since the end of the Second World War. The historically most important may have been 1969's May 13 incident in Malaysia and Indonesia's anti-Chinese riots during the late 1990s Asian financial crisis. Both were brutal, widespread, and deadly. In the Philippines, the Spanish colonialists were more hostile to Chinese immigrants than native Filipinos have ever been, and compared to Malaysia and Indonesia, Chinese Filipinos are more assimilated into Filipino culture. Thailand has, mercifully, overwhelmingly avoided anti-Chinese violence in the last fifty years, and assimilation through marriage is quite common. National experiences with ethnic diversity are diverse.

Chinese Immigrants: Market-Creating Minorities

Across Southeast Asia, the countries with the most Chinese immigrants have been the most prosperous overall—for Chinese and non-Chinese citizens alike. On average, ethnic Malays in Malaysia are far more prosperous than ethnic Filipinos in the Philippines, and ethnic Thais and Indonesians are somewhere in the middle. At least as a matter of correlation, of historical patterns, it's great to be in a Southeast Asian country with a lot of Chinese immigrants— the more the better.

But how much of this is a matter of cause and effect? As usual in the study of society, there are no true experiments. But statistical methods can once again help us compare apples with apples and ask, "If I look at two countries that are outwardly similar, but one has quite a lot more Chinese immigrants, does the economy with more Chinese immigrants grow a lot faster?"

Economists Jan Priebe of Goettingen in Germany and Robert Rudolf of Korea University in Seoul tried to ask just that question.

The title of their article is "Does the Chinese Diaspora Speed Up Growth in Host Countries?" Their question is important one: "We examine whether countries grow faster if their population comprises a larger share of overseas Chinese."[12]

After trying to compare apples with apples—by looking at countries with similar geography, starting levels of education, and so on, what do they find? A "country's initial [number of] overseas Chinese is positively related to subsequent growth."[13]

So, they're confirming the same pattern we saw informally earlier. But since economists like to know why a relationship exists, they went further and checked to see how economies with a lot of Chinese immigrants were different from other economies:

> The presence of overseas Chinese contributes to a country's participation in international trade, [faster growth in machines, equipment, and factories], and increased . . . productivity, which in turn all stimulate growth.[14]

The authors, like many who study Southeast Asia, draw on the evidence for cultural differences as well:

> According to some scholars overseas Chinese are characterized by a comparatively strong emphasis on family economic success, including long working hours, thrifty and dynamic family businesses, and a high emphasis on educating the next generation. These cultural traits, if large enough to leave their footprint on a whole society, might have repercussions for . . . a country's economy.[15]

So how much do overseas Chinese appear to matter for a nation's economy? Using cross-country data from 1970 to 2010, Priebe and Rudolf find that a 10 percentage point increase in a nation's Chinese share of the population predicts that the nation would grow 0.7 percent faster per year, year after year. Because of compounding, that would mean a nation where 10 percent of the population had Chinese ancestors would be 10 percent richer in a decade compared to a similar nation that had zero citizens with Chinese ancestry. And taken literally (don't take it literally!), it would mean that China itself should grow 7 percent faster per year than otherwise similar nations without any Chinese immigrants—countries with the same education level, fraction that are immigrants, same population density, similar geography—the usual.

That might sound unrealistically high until you realize that from the death of Mao until 2010, incomes per person in China grew about 8.5 percent per year according to the World Bank, an astonishingly high rate, especially for such a long period. During that same time, the average income in the typical country grew 2 percent per year—a 6.5 percent annual gap—so China's experience isn't that far from what you'd predict from Priebe and Rudolf's research.

You might ask yourself whether they found such a strong link because their statistical analysis includes China itself in the average. But it doesn't. The authors intentionally omitted China, Taiwan, Hong Kong, and Macau. This is a study of China that includes data from 147 countries but includes only one majority-Chinese country (you can guess which), so there's no way for Chinese-majority countries to skew the results.

Chinese Immigrants: Building the Capitalist Road

Are the cultural traits that Chinese migrants bring shaping the governments in the countries they move to? Let's look this time at the Economic Freedom of the World index published by the libertarian Cato Institute,[16] and bring in both the Chinese share of the population and the migration-adjusted Tech Index (see table 7.3). With the exception of Thailand, the pattern we've seen in chapter 4 holds up: ancestral excellence in technology strongly predicts a modern, market-friendly economy. And you'll recall that Thailand is actually quite a bit richer than the Philippines and Indonesia—countries with lower Economic Freedom scores, so this may be a case where the proof of the pudding is in the dollars and not in the Economic Freedom rating.

And majority-Chinese Hong Kong and Singapore are nearly always at the top of any cross-country index of pro-market policies, another reminder that the capitalist road that Mao feared has expanded far beyond mainland China.

But consider the case of Malaysia: relatively market-friendly, but

TABLE 7.3. Chinese ancestry, Tech History, and Economic Freedom across Southeast Asia.

	Population of Chinese descent, 1980	Migration-adjusted tech index, 1500	Economic freedom rating, 2018, Cato
Philippines	2%	0.58	7.4
Indonesia	4%	0.66	7.4
Thailand	10%	0.77	6.8
Malaysia	33%	0.76	7.6
Singapore	77%	0.84	8.7
Hong Kong	98%	0.88	8.9

Sources: Rauch and Trindade (2002); Comin, Easterly, and Gong (2010); Gwartney et al. (2018).

with Economic Freedom scores a bit above the Philippines and Indonesia. Is it plausible that having a sizable market-dominant minority, as Malaysia does, can actually make a nation's government more market-friendly?

Yes, but not because it means members of the market-dominant minority are welcomed into top positions in government. Malaysia, like Indonesia and the Philippines, almost never has top government officials of Chinese descent—though Malaysia did briefly have a finance minister of Chinese descent, Lim Guan Eng, from mid-2018 to early 2020. Discrimination and in particular Sinophobia, both overt and subtle, keep Chinese migrants disproportionately out of government in the very countries they have helped to enrich. So, the presence of Chinese immigrants in government isn't what's building the capitalist road.

Instead, consider this possibility: governments typically aren't wild about embracing market-friendly policies, but when they see that a sizable market-dominant minority could grow even more prosperous if the government embraced markets just a little more, that makes the government a lot more likely to push for markets. That's partly because when the market-dominant minority becomes more prosperous, there's more revenue that the government can tax. By contrast, a nation with weaker market prospects—perhaps because it has few if any citizens who are members of market-dominant minorities—then it isn't as excited about reform. That's because even if they get the reforms right, there'll be a much smaller pot of gold at the end of the economic reform rainbow. Pro-market economic reform is hard, and the promise of massive prosperity is one of the few reasons to make the heavy lift.

So, the prospect of a bigger tax base alone—let alone the prospect of greater prosperity for the masses—can nudge a government toward market friendly reforms. And if there's one thing that market-dominant minorities can create, it's a bigger tax base, a bigger pot of gold for the government to distribute to others.

This is just a theory, but it's a theory that can help explain a puzzle we see across Southeast Asia: the fact that overall, the presence of more Chinese migrants predicts more broad-based prosperity. And if the theory is true, it means that one way to spur governments to embrace pro-market reforms is to encourage those countries to admit more market-dominant minorities as long-term, multigenerational immigrants. The world's poorest nations, those with the weakest support for competition and markets, would, I believe, dramatically improve their economic chances if they were able to encourage enough Chinese immigration.

The next time you see an ad that asks you to contribute cash to fight poverty in a desperately poor country, I hope you ask yourself these questions:

Shouldn't I, perhaps, make it easier for Chinese people to immigrate to that country?

Shouldn't I encourage that country to schedule an appointment for a culture transplant—to welcome market-dominant, market-creating minorities?

What about Other Southeast Asian Countries?

I've left off quite a few countries in Southeast Asia. Consider some countries in the region with a sizable number of Chinese immigrants:

Vietnam: Around 10 percent Chinese—a group typically known as the Hoa people—and like China, getting over the big mistake of communism rapidly. Their income today doesn't tell us all that much about their long-run prospects. Poorer today than the Philippines but growing much more quickly. A former French colony.

Myanmar (formerly Burma): A national socialist military dictatorship until (officially at least) 2011. Think of Myanmar as taking a uniquely bad path to communism and now trying to find a path away from it, though the economy is still heavily dominated by the military. A poor country by any measure, though not among the very poorest, with incomes around the level of Honduras or Nicaragua or Nigeria. Perhaps 3 percent of the population has Chinese ancestry. A former British colony.

Laos: The Laotian Chinese community makes up perhaps 2 percent of the population of the country. The headline from a 1964 article in the *New York Times* tells an all-too-common story: "Chinese Are Thriving in Laos, but the Community Is Resented."[17] Incomes are about the same as in the Philippines. Like Vietnam, a former French colony.

Cambodia: The Khmer Rouge targeted capitalists—typically, just successful businesspeople—for murder and persecution, and since the Chinese immigrants here as in so many other countries were a market-dominant minority, their numbers dwindled in the 1970s and 1980s. Estimates vary of the number of Chinese Cambodians today, but 0.1–3 percent is a range worth thinking about. Still poor, quite a bit poorer than Myanmar and far below the Philippines or Laos. Like Laos and Vietnam, once a French colony.

I ask you to remember the 1.5 to 2 million people mur-
dered in the Khmer Rouge genocide, which targeted people
who had any signs of excellence or intellectual vigor. If you
wear eyeglasses, like I do, you would have been a potential
target for their slaughters.

Brunei: The only country in Southeast Asia that both has high
incomes and a non-Chinese majority. Instead, Brunei has oil.

Southeast Asia: A Test of the Assimilation Myth

Over the years, I've often been told that migrants change a nation's
government only when they arrive violently, with guns and germs
and steel. Migrants who arrive peacefully, it is said, never change
the governments or the national economies in the places they move
to. They might bring some new ethnic cuisines, some new words
might enter the language, but that'll be about it. Otherwise, life
will overwhelmingly be as before for the rest of the nation's residents, even generations later.

But Southeast Asia's Chinese diaspora disproves all of that. They
arrived peacefully, and though there were many exceptions, on average, members of the diaspora grew to have well-deserved but disproportionate wealth and control over the private sector. And either
directly, as in Singapore, or indirectly (as I argue), as in Malaysia,
they shaped the government's attitude toward markets. If peaceful migration changes your nation's migration-adjusted SAT score,
there's strong reason to believe that over the decades, your nation's
government institutions and your nation's income per person will
be shaped as a result.

Further, the diaspora is a strong—perhaps even an extreme—
example of the persistence of cultural traits across generations. For
Southeast Asia as a whole, full immigrant assimilation is a myth.
In most countries, Chinese migrants have for centuries tended to
retain the language and cultural traditions of their homelands,
even if there's been drift and fusion and accommodation over time.

There are exceptions—Thailand is the biggest exception, where cultural assimilation of Chinese migrants has been relatively strong by regional standards—but we should base policy on the general rule. And the general rule is cultural persistence; the general rule is not full assimilation.

And the diaspora is, horrifyingly, an example of the costs of ethnic diversity. These are costs worth dwelling upon with real candor. I think these costs are worth paying for Southeast Asian countries, because I believe the prospect of better economies—which means better health care, greater human flourishing, and less drudgery—is worth the very real risk of Indonesia-style pogroms and deadly ethnic riots. The many lives, including young lives, that would be dramatically extended over the next half century if Indonesia's 300 million citizens became twice as rich are, in my personal estimation, worth the genuine risk of an ethnic riot every decade that kills two thousand people.

The infant mortality rate in Indonesia is four times higher than in France, and average lifespans in Indonesia are ten years shorter than in Australia. In the poor countries of the world, particularly the poorest, the benefits of massively greater immigration from China would massively and obviously outweigh the costs of ethnic diversity, including the risk of violent ethnic conflict.

This is not an easy judgment to come to, but any immigration policy involves cruel trade-offs. This is my personal judgment, and I encourage you to come to your own judgment. I hope that experts can find ways to reduce ethnic conflict, defuse it, eliminate it—but I can't await a cure to such a chronic social ailment. Instead, I need to offer the best policy advice that will improve lives today, this year, this coming half century, with the biggest benefits and the lowest costs.

And my prescription is clear: *Expand the Chinese diaspora.*

Millions of Chinese immigrants have already moved to developing countries in the last few decades, and not just in Southeast Asia. *New York Times* reporter Howard French's excellent book *China's Second Continent: How a Million Migrants Are Building a New Empire in Africa* gives away the plot with its title.[18] China is uniquely important as a potential source of voluntary high-SAT immigrants because China combines a massive population with relatively low-enough average incomes. For at least another twenty years, it's just possible to imagine poor nations giving a ten-year tax amnesty to long-term immigrants from China, or to imagine philanthropic movements choosing to subsidize long-term peaceful, voluntary migration from China to some of the world's poorest countries.

There are a lot of plans out there to end poverty in poor countries. Here's mine: *More migration along the capitalist road.*

8 The Deep Roots across the Fifty United States

What impact on local development do immigrants and their descendants have in the short and long term? The answer depends on the attributes they bring with them, what they pass on to their children, and how they interact with other groups.

—Scott Fulford, Ivan Petkov, and Fabio Schiantarelli,
  Journal of Economic Growth, 2020[1]

AMERICA IS A NATION OF IMMIGRANTS.

Of course, every nation is a nation of immigrants since humans have moved into and out of every nation in the world. But America is different from most countries: in the vast majority of cases, when immigrants arrived in America, those arrivals were documented, counted, recorded. The people we call indigenous or Native Americans weren't literally indigenous to North America; instead, they're the people whose ancestors arrived in prehistory, before accountants and government recorders and slave traders could tally the arrivals. The Native Americans are immigrants too.

So, if America is particularly a nation of immigrants, it is only because America is a nation of documents. And those documents offer a final way to test the cultural transplant theory of economic development, the theory that behavioral traits, transmitted persistently if imperfectly across generations, dramatically shape national economies.

Economist Scott Fulford and his coauthors Ivan Petkov and Fabio Schiantarelli recently tested the cultural transplant theory in a way we haven't seen. They looked at over a thousand U.S. counties to see if the ancestral background of a county's residents predicted average economic productivity and average income in the county. Now you might think this is a trivial task, worth nobody's time; it's well known that in the modern U.S., Asians on average earn more than whites, who on average earn more than Latinos, who on average earn more than Americans of African descent. But they checked for that—in part by running a comparison between their ancestry measures and simple measures of "race." And even knowing the racial demographics of a county, Fulford, Petkov, and Schiantarelli found that knowing the specific national ancestry of a county's residents—Swiss or Mexican or Czech or Polish or Italian and so on—still helps predict average incomes today in that county.

Going further, Fulford—from here onward, I'll just refer to the first author—found that average modern incomes in the ancestral homeland help predict average modern county incomes today. This clever test works a lot like the cultural persistence tests of Algan and Cahuc and Alesina and Giuliano that we saw in chapter 1. While those papers compared cultural attitudes of Italian Americans to Italians in modern Italy, Fulford compared incomes of a 100-percent Italian American county to incomes in modern Italy. More realistically—since there are no 100-percent Italian American counties in the U.S.—he compared the average incomes in a county to the average incomes of a hypothetical country with the same ancestral background. A county that's 80 percent Swedish American, 10 percent British American, and 10 percent Mexican American gets compared to a weighted average of incomes in Sweden, Britain, and Mexico, with almost all of the weight put on Sweden. Fulford does that about 18,000 times—once for each U.S. county for which there's good data, and once for every decade from 1850 to 2010. So, this paper doesn't just have data from different locations; it also has data from different decades.

Three examples that fit the basic story: Norwegians earn more than Poles, who earn more than Filipinos on average in their home countries, and a hypothetical U.S. county that was 100 percent Norwegian would produce more than a county that was 100 percent Polish, which in turn would produce more than a county that was 100 percent Filipino. As always, there are exceptions to the rule—French Americans earn a lot more than you'd expect by looking at incomes in France, and Austrian Americans earn a bit less. Exceptions bend but don't break this general rule: ancestral homes help predict county incomes and county productivity. Fulford finds that a little more than half—56 percent—of county's modern productivity looks like it's transmitted from the old country to the new county.

Not bad for such a simple, incomplete measure of ancestry. Once again, immigrants import their economic destiny, to a large extent, from their ancestral homelands.

Immigrants from Rich Countries: Just Picking the Good Real Estate?

Tests of cultural transplant theory in the U.S. return us to the same questions we asked when we looked at the world as a whole: What if immigrants from, say, Norway just bought (or stole) the good places first, and what if immigrants from, say, the Philippines wound up in bad locations due to fate or oppression? What if these cultural measures are mostly hiding a story about geography?

Because Fulford has data running from the Civil War era to the global financial crisis era, and because these data include both U.S. Census information on ancestry as well as estimates of each county's average income, he can check whether what looks like ancestry is really just a matter of location—or even a matter of a county's population density or average education levels. Better-educated people tend to produce more, as do people in denser locations, so these are good possibilities to check.

And ancestry passes the test with flying colors. That holds true even when you statistically set aside African-Americans and Native

Americans—whose ancestors suffered unique horrors within the United States that may distort the Fulford results—and instead only look at other differences in ancestry.

In addition, geography itself can't destroy the results either. Indeed, all of the paper's central results treat each county as its own unique geography, known as the "county fixed effect," so if there's just been something special about New York City since 1850 (and there has!) and if that were the only reason for the high incomes of some immigrant groups, then Fulford's tests could tell us that (but they didn't). There's a lot of geographical tire kicking in the paper—and together it points toward the predictive power of ancestry.

What Is Ancestry Predicting?

Fulford showed that people's national ancestry matters—but then he goes further and asks why. In particular, he checks whether most or even all the power of national ancestry is a shorthand for three big measures we've already seen:

Home-country average cultural traits, including trust (chapter 1)

Home-country values for the Putterman-Weil State History index (chapter 2)

Home-country measures of constraints on the government executive (chapter 4)

Individually, each of these measures helps predict a county's income level—little surprise, since they all are useful in predicting national prosperity. But when they run horse races between these Deep Roots measures, Putterman-Weil's State History measure comes in first, culture comes in second, and executive constraints are far behind.

So, a simple index of ancestral experience living under organized states was the big winner—an index that, as we've seen, tends to lose out to the Tech History index. It's like learning that Aquaman defeated a supervillain. If even he could beat the Big Bad, that's a good sign the Man of Steel wouldn't even have had to break a sweat.

And it's important to emphasize a point that Fulford makes, one that applies to all the ancestry-based measures used throughout this book: these measures all hide an enormous amount of variation within each ancestral group. Fulford notes, for example, that his measure of Russian ancestry necessarily combines Orthodox Christian Russians with Jewish Russians—it's the nature of statistics to simplify, and he's simplifying at the level of the nation. In a related way, we should remember that the measure of immigrants from France combines French medical doctors who came to America so they could earn more money and French high school graduates who came on vacation and never got around to leaving. And by the way, the latter is too big to ignore: about half a percent of all 2 million French arrivals to the U.S end up overstaying their visas, whether they came for tourism or school, for a total of around 10,000 people every year.[2] That might not sound like much until you realize that only about 3,000 French people become U.S. citizens each year.[3]

So, the diversity of immigrants within each country is surely very important—and while education is the easiest way to capture that, there's still a difference between a master's in medieval history and a master's in electrical engineering. Both are great—but the latter has a lot bigger chance of increasing the world's stock of useful knowledge. And the fact that these imperfect proxies, these ancestral shortcuts, are doing such a good job predicting American outcomes is a sign that better proxies would do an ever better job.

We're finding a lot of low-hanging fruit in the Deep Roots literature—as each chapter you've read has demonstrated. That's one reason why so many economists have been diving into this particular research orchard. By the time you read this, there will surely be many new findings on the links connecting ancestry, migration, and modern outcomes, but based on the track record so far, future work won't be refuting these results. Future work will be extending them.

Firefly versus Value Diversity: An American Test

We've seen evidence that two kinds of diversity surely matter for prosperity: diversity of skills and diversity of values. The business literature finds lots of evidence that skill diversity helps a company to succeed—a form of diversity I called *Firefly* diversity, after the TV series with a motley crew whose members have wildly varying skills but who still come together in the end. And separately, cross-country research found that when people with different ethnic backgrounds tend to also have different cultural attitudes, that is a real predictor of social conflict and of a great chance for civil war. To simplify a vast and ongoing research project:

Skill diversity: Good for national flourishing

Ethnic diversity combined with cultural value diversity: A higher risk of destructive social conflict

Fulford uses U.S. counties to test key elements of both of these predictions. What does he find? He phrases it politely, a good idea on such a sensitive topic:

It seems that when groups have to share a place and work together, diversity is good, as long as there is a degree of agreement in terms of cultural attitudes that facilitate exchange, production, and the ability to agree in the public sphere.[4]

Literally, what Fulford finds is that greater ancestry diversity within a county predicts more prosperity, whereas greater value diversity within a county predicts less prosperity. This message is a little more optimistic than what we saw across countries earlier. At least within U.S. counties, more ancestral diversity is good news, in the range we've seen in the U.S. over the last 160 years, and that's true even without knowing whether those groups differ in cultural values. It's a little like knowing that heavier people are stronger on average—the weight may or may not make them strong, but it predicts other good traits (height, muscle mass) that help make a person stronger.

But once we have a measure of cultural values, the message flips: greater cultural value diversity in a county doesn't predict economic strength in that county; it predicts economic weakness. Much of the explanation might be as simple as Fulford suggests in the quote. Maybe cultural disagreement just makes it harder for businesses and schools and non-profits and governments to cooperate on big, high-value projects. Other explanations are possible. Maybe the whole story is that government leaders from the dominant ethnic group discriminate against culturally diverse regions, putting the good roads and good schoolteachers elsewhere.

One paper alone can't settle the issue, but we don't have just one paper. Instead, we have a vast empirical literature using a variety of methods. It's time to notice the general pattern across business research, cross-country research, and within-country research that cultural diversity is a source of social frictions big enough, it appears, to hurt productivity, wages, incomes, and tranquility. If we could have the kind of ancestry diversity that optimists hope for— where we all come from different countries but deep down all share similar values—then we can return to the fully optimistic story where our diversity is our strength. I hope we arrive at that promised land—but I don't think anyone has directions to get there.

Importing America's Future Values

Two of the same authors—Petkov of Northeastern University and Schiantarelli of Boston College—joined Francesco Giavazzi of Italy's famed Bocconi University to tell another story about America.[5] Giavazzi—from here onward, I'll just refer to the new author—ran a uniquely sophisticated test of whether and how long the cultural traits of immigrants who come to America persist. Giavazzi focused on immigrants and their second-generation and fourth-generation descendants—their children and their great-grandchildren—from seven big cultural groups:

Great Britain

Germany

Ireland

Italy

Poland

Scandinavia (Sweden, Denmark, Norway, Finland)

Mexico

And Giavazzi looked at eight big sets of cultural attitudes—all but one of which draw on multiple survey questions, and most of which average together three or more survey questions. The eight attitudes, with some of the related questions, are these:

1. Cooperation (The trust question: are people usually fair and helpful?)

2. Role of government (Should government create more equality? Are you Left or Right?)

3. Religiosity (Do you pray regularly, attend a religious service? Is there an afterlife?)

4. Family (Should you obey your parents? Should it be easy to get divorced?)

5. Gender roles (Should women work outside the home when children are small?)

6. Abortion (Is abortion acceptable without any restrictions?)

7. Sexual behavior (What are your views on premarital sex and homosexuality?)

8. Mobility and getting ahead in life (Can you get ahead if you try hard?)

In the big picture, pulling all groups of immigrants and their descendants together, the second generation is less than 50 percent convergent in six of the eight categories. The two biggest topics for convergence: mobility, with 57 percent convergence, and abortion attitudes, with exactly 50–50 convergence. Cooperation is the area with the least convergence in the second generation—just 33 percent of the way. All the others are between 43 percent and 46 percent. The children of immigrants are mostly holding old-country attitudes.

By the fourth generation, after scores of years in America, have immigrants finally assimilated? Or have they at least, say, 90 percent assimilated? Nope. The overall highest rate of assimilation is 81 percent—fortunately, on cooperation. That means that on average, fourth-generation immigrants closed 81 percent of the gap between views in the old country and views in the United States. That's more trust assimilation than we saw in chapter 1, but note that this is just looking at these seven big cultural groups, and so it's leaving out a lot of Americans. The lowest degree of assimilation is, alas, on the role of government—not great news if you think immigrants will overwhelmingly adopt the political opinions that are common in the country they move to. My colleague at George Mason, Bryan Caplan, has argued that immigrants are likely to conform to typical American attitudes, since people overall are conformists. Recall his words quoted in chapter 1: "If people have a generic tendency to prefer what already exists, admitting them to a more libertarian society effectively makes them more libertarian: 'Liberty is what you already have here. Fine, let's stick with that.'"

And since America works pretty well compared to the countries immigrants have come from, he makes the case that we should expect a lot of political conformity: Caplan argues that the view that "people who come here will largely accept our status quo as long as it more or less works" is "realism."[6]

Compared to most real-world countries, America works pretty well, so it seems to be a good test case for Caplan's theory. So, how much do fourth-generation immigrants conform to the views of the average American on the proper role of government?

A mere 38 percent by Giavazzi's estimates. That's actually less than in the second generation! He found that the second generation closed 43 percent of the government attitude gap between the old country and the average American. Overall, that low level of conformity is a bad sign, unless you think most immigrants come from countries with better political attitudes than Americans currently have. If it turned out that most of America's immigrants came from prosperous, market-friendly Singapore, I'd be open to that argument—but in reality we should probably be skeptical about claims that the last few generations of immigrants, on average, came from countries with better views on economic policy. Caplan's allegedly realistic position isn't looking like the evidence-based position.

Overall, across all eight attitudes, Giavazzi finds that a bit less than 60 percent of the attitude gap is closed by the fourth generation. Full assimilation, even 90 percent assimilation, once again appears to be a myth.

Those results pull all seven big cultural groups together, but Giavazzi also breaks them apart. Across all twenty-four survey questions, Giavazzi reports the percentage of the questions where at least half the gap closes between home-country and fourth-generation attitudes. So, 50-percent assimilation is his cutoff—so he's grading on a very generous curve. By this measure, the biggest conformers to average American attitudes are German immigrants. They converge at least halfway on 79 percent of the questions by the fourth generation. The least conforming are Polish immigrants, mostly conforming on just 38 percent of the questions. Everyone else is in the middle:

Irish	67 percent
British	67 percent
Mexicans	58 percent
Italians	58 percent
Scandinavians	54 percent

For the issues we've usually focused on when thinking about prosperity—views on cooperation and the role of government—the pattern holds up as well across the seven cultural groups: Germans mostly conform on five out of six questions; Mexicans and Poles on two of six; Italians on three; and Scandinavians, Irish, and the British on four of six.

Giavazzi notices these differences in persistence: "Persistence is also country specific, in the sense that the country of origin of one's ancestors matters for the pattern of generational convergence."[7]

It's not just that cultural attitudes differ across countries and cultures. In addition, at least in the U.S. over the last century, the *persistence* of attitudes has differed substantially as well. Some cultures conformed more, some less, but no culture is conforming 90 percent of the way to typical American views. Let's hope that the ones who are conforming less are importing cultural traits America needs more of.

The Worst You Could Say

The Cato Institute is a free-market, libertarian-leaning think tank in Washington, D.C. It's been kind enough to have me on their daily podcast a couple of times, and I admire many of the great people there; their roster of thinkers and writers includes many who are truly skilled and thoughtful. As a rule, they tend to be extremely supportive of more immigration from every country, and some of their scholars write papers arguing that the benefits of immigration are underrated and the costs overrated.

In the last few years, as the Deep Roots literature has grown in prominence, Cato's Alex Nowrasteh has jumped into the Deep Roots debate, with a number of critiques of the literature. His critiques have yet to find resonance in academic circles—a coauthored paper that dismisses scholarly research on trust is one example[8]—but I give him credit for trying.

Nowrasteh recently coauthored a paper that looked at the Deep Roots across the fifty states—so it has something in common with Fulford's paper.[9] But instead of looking at America's three thousand counties, Cato's Nowrasteh and Southern Methodist University's Ryan Murphy looked at the fifty U.S. states; but as elsewhere, I'll refer just to the first author, Nowrasteh. Instead of using the variety of predictors Fulford used—cultural, income-based, and ancestral—Nowrasteh used just the S and A in the SAT score: State History and Agricultural History. You'll recall that they are two of the weakest predictors of national prosperity and of national government quality; Nowrasteh checked whether state-level differences in S and A scores could predict differences in outcomes across the fifty states.

So, what did he find?

At the most basic level, he found that S and A earned maybe a B- in predicting differences in income across the U.S. states. Yes, more of each looks better for prosperity as rule, but it turns out that in simple horse races, regional differences in climate across the states beat out S and A. This isn't much of a surprise—and note that he never included T, the more powerful Tech History predictor, in his tests. But then Nowrasteh chose to add a new horse to the race: the percent of each state's population that is non-Hispanic white, or NHW, as scholars in the field often say. It turns out that more NHWs predict lower income on average. My guess as to why: across American history, people of all races and ethnic backgrounds have tended to move to prosperous places. And certainly, since the Second World War if not before, much of that migration to great places has been by non-NHWs—mostly by people with African, Hispanic, and Asian ancestry. So, the negative relationship he finds might just be telling us that some states aren't attractive places to move to. Sometimes geography really drives outcomes—and those Wisconsin winters are never going to be an immigration magnet.

In any case, once Nowrasteh puts NHW into the horse race, things change: higher S and A scores now reliably predict more state-level prosperity, and the relationship is usually strong and relatively precise. It doesn't look like noise; it doesn't appear to be a mere coincidence. In their simple test across the fifty states, there's good evidence—but not ironclad—that longer ancestral experience living under organized states and more ancestral experience with formal agriculture predict higher state-level incomes. If that's what a hostile critic of the Deep Roots literature is finding, what should an impartial observer believe?

Nowrasteh goes further, running additional tests to see if higher S and A scores predict fewer government convictions for political corruption, more social capital, and more legal protections for personal and economic freedom. He also includes some basic measures of geography in the horse race so that there's a little bit of competition to predict these outcomes. He finds that higher State History and higher Agricultural History scores predict lower government corruption, more social capital, and more income equality; in addition, higher State History scores predict more state-level legal protections for overall personal and economic freedom. Nowrasteh finds much noisier relationships between the Deep Roots scores and some other state-level outcomes, but the direction of the relationship almost always points in the direction we'd expect based on the patterns between SAT scores and institutional quality we saw in chapter 4. Overall, he finds that greater ancestral experience living under organized states or using sophisticated agricultural methods predicts better outcomes. If this is a debunking of the Deep Roots literature, I welcome more such debunkings.

Smart, careful critics can help us test our theories. The adversarial approach to finding truth—where each faction tries to critique and debunk the claims of the other factions—works well in the courtroom and it works well in economics. That means that Nowrasteh's critique can serve as our final answer to that most crucial of questions: is the past prologue?

On average, the answer appears to be yes—as long as you adjust for migration.

→Je ne sais quoi←

Among the biological and cultural baggage that Europeans brought to their colonies, which elements contributed to the consequences of large European immigration?

—Jared Diamond, "Reversals of National Fortune, and Social Science Methodologies," 2014[1]

MEDICAL EXPERTS PRESCRIBED ASPIRIN FOR TWO hundred years without knowing why it worked. The story of aspirin starts in 1763, when the Reverend Edward Stone presented the British Royal Society with "An Account of the Success of the Bark of the Willow in the Cure of Agues."[2] *Ague* was that era's word for fever and chills. The reverend claims he "accidentally" tasted the willow bark—a likely story! He immediately noticed it had the same bitter taste as Peruvian bark, a source of quinine, the famed treatment for malaria. That simple parallel, that analogous taste, was enough to spur him to "make some experiments with it; and, for this purpose, I gathered that summer near a pound weight of [willow bark], which I dried in a bag . . . for more than three months, at which time it was to be reduced to a powder . . . and . . . pulverized."

When Stone later had a malaria-like fever, he took some of the powder, gradually boosting the dose, and saw that the fever weakened and then vanished. Then he found some human guinea pigs:

"It was then given to several others with the same success." And after five years of testing, having given it to about fifty people, he concluded that dried, ground willow bark worked, so he wrote to the Royal Society to let them know. And that's how we learned about the drug we now call aspirin.

There are a lot of loose stories floating about online and in books claiming that the ancient Greek thinker Hippocrates figured out that chewing on willow bark or drinking willow bark tea could cure fevers. But as pharmacologist Philippa Martyr of the University of Western Australia has noted, those are urban legends. In reality, Hippocrates's only clear discussion of willow involved women smoking willow leaves—not the bark—to avoid complications during a miscarriage.[3] The clear history of willow bark as a fever reducer begins with Stone's letter to the Royal Society, and it began with experiments.

But there's one big limitation to the experimental method: it can show that a treatment works, but by itself an experiment doesn't show why a treatment works. This is a limitation—to call it a problem would be an overstatement—of any situation where a treatment group is given a new medicine and a control group, a placebo group, isn't.

People love to hear a why, an explanation for how a new medical treatment, an immigration policy, or a new teaching method works. People love a theory; they love a good story. But as my George Mason University colleague Tyler Cowen suggested in a long-ago TEDx talk, we should "be suspicious of simple stories."[4] It's easy to make up a story—which means the cost of storytelling is low. And human beings just love to hear stories—so the demand is high for stories, especially for stories that feel real. High demand and low cost of production: it doesn't take a Ph.D. in economics to safely predict that we'll see a lot of stories that feel real, whether or not those stories are true.

So, it's no surprise that Reverend Stone had an intuitive, reasonable-to-his-audience story for why the willow bark might cure malaria-like fevers:

> As this [willow] tree delights in a moist or wet soil, where agues [malaria-like fevers and chills] chiefly abound, the general maxim, that many natural maladies carry their cures along with them, or that their remedies lie not far from their causes, was so very [appropriate] to this particular case, that I could not help applying it.

So, the good reverend went with a sort of nature-points-in-the-right-direction theory of pharmacological geography. He drew upon his professional training in theology as well: "That this might be the intention of Providence here, I must own had some little weight with me."

Together, those two stories, those intuitive explanations, made up Stone's theory for why dehydrated, pulverized willow bark cured fevers. A bad pair of explanations, but bad explanations were the only ones on offer at the time.

And for two hundred years, the story didn't improve much. It was only in 1971, two centuries after Stone published his essay, that John Vane discovered exactly how acetylsalicylic acid—the real name for aspirin—actually worked inside the human body. Vane discovered what was known as aspirin's "mechanism of action." He eventually shared a Nobel prize for his discovery. And notice: it took two centuries to progress from the what to the true why.

How Culture Is Transplanted

Obviously, the story of aspirin is a metaphor for the cultural transplant channels we've investigated. We know pretty clearly that culture persists and that culture substantially survives migration, but we really don't know exactly why it persists. As we head into the middle of the twenty-first century, that's the state of knowledge on the crucial role that culture plays in national economies: it's like a lab experiment where we can be relatively confident that correlation really is causation, but we can't be at all sure where the causation really comes from. We can't be sure why cultural traits are so persistent. Culture today is a lot like aspirin in 1800.

Are group cultural differences 100 percent genetic? Are they 100 percent teachable and easily changeable, something fixable with some regular public service announcements on Facebook? Or instead, is there a third option, that culture is a set of switchable focal points, social norms that are hard for one person to change alone but fairly easy to change if we all do it at once? In other words, are cultural norms a lot like deciding which side of the street to drive on?

If the focal-point theory turned out to be true, then in principle there might be some way for everyone in a culture to switch to better, more productive cultural norms, just a little like the way that Swedes all switched from driving on the left-hand side of the road to the right-hand side of the road on 1967's famous H Day. On H day—September 3—at 4:50 p.m., everyone in Sweden stopped their vehicle and had ten minutes to move their cars to the other side of the road. Then, at 5:00 p.m., they all started driving for the first time ever—simultaneously—on the right-hand side. Perhaps some bigger, much more important cultural reforms could work like that—even some of the most important ones. Or perhaps, cultural persistence is created through some synthesis of two or three of these channels: genetic, individual learned norms, and group focal-point norms. Perhaps different channels matter more for different cultural traits.

But all of that is speculative. And those few sentences represent only the beginnings of a wide range of possibilities for future speculation. Indeed, anything I might write about the why of cultural persistence would be purely speculative. This hasn't been a book with a lot of speculation, and it's not going to turn into one now: I leave the speculation to future researchers.

Economists are used to this distinction between showing *that* X causes Y versus showing *why* X causes Y. The great philosopher David Hume wrote in the 1700s that an increase in the supply of money caused the economy to grow faster for a while, but we've spent over two hundred years debating why—indeed, my doctoral dissertation was about a small piece of that massive puzzle.

Is it because businesses are confused by the sudden rise in prices, thinking that their goods are temporarily more popular? Or does money growth cause a boost in output because prices take a while to adjust, and so consumers feel richer for a while? There's at least one Nobel prize on each side of that claim: Robert Lucas for the former and Edmund Phelps for the latter story.

Similarly, we know that receiving a college diploma causes you as an individual to earn more money on average, but is that mostly because the diploma is just a reliable signal that you were already smart, or is it mostly because you learned things in college that actually made you more useful? Each of those two theories won Nobel prizes: one to Michael Spence and one to Gary Becker.

So, knowing the that is different, and often quite separate, from knowing the why. But the that is no small thing. Good economic policy, good immigration policy, can be built on a foundation of thats. After all, we still don't know why acetaminophen—often known as Tylenol—can make many headaches and fevers go away. Yes, we now know the mechanism of action for aspirin, but the mechanism of action for Tylenol is still widely debated. However, that ignorance doesn't prevent doctors from considering Tylenol an extremely safe medicine, safe enough to prescribe routinely.

What makes Tylenol work? What process ensures that migrants make the economies they move to a lot like the ones they left?

As the French say, "I don't know what."

The Goose and the Golden Eggs

There was once a Countryman who possessed the most wonderful Goose you can imagine, for every day when he visited the nest, the Goose had laid a beautiful, glittering, golden egg.

The Countryman took the eggs to market and soon began to get rich. But it was not long before he grew impatient with the Goose because she gave him only a single golden egg a day. He was not getting rich fast enough.

Then one day, after he had finished counting his money, the idea came to him that he could get all the golden eggs at once by killing the Goose and cutting it open. But when the deed was done, not a single golden egg did he find, and his precious Goose was dead.

—"The Goose and the Golden Egg," *The Æsop for Children,* 1919[1]

FABLES ARE A LOT LIKE ECONOMIC THEORIES. Both are types of stories that, at their best, teach us part of the true nature of the world around us. Aesop's story of the goose who could lay eggs of solid gold tells us that wealth is created by a mysterious process—by something inside the goose, hard to see, harder to understand, impossible to replicate.

The wealth of nations is produced in a similarly mysterious process—and more of it is produced in some countries than in others. Why do some nations produce twenty or thirty times more output per person than other nations? Many are tempted to look for explanations that are convenient but that do little to explain the puzzle. Maybe the wealth is inside the goose! Maybe it's latitude! Or Christianity! Or exploitation!

Many more are tempted to think only about the short run. Why not cut the goose open now and get whatever you can! Seize the day! There's no time like the present!

And when the problem of human poverty is so pressing, with well over half a billion people on earth living on less than $2 a day, with over 2 billion people without basic toilets or latrines, and over fifty countries where the average lifespan is below seventy, it's easy to see why it's so appealing, so intuitive, to press for greater immigration from the poorest countries to the richest ones. In the short run—a couple of decades, say—admitting an extra ten million people each year from the world's poorest nations into the high-innovation I-7 nations would surely improve the lives of almost every immigrant. After all, government and culture rarely change much in the short run.

But in the longer run, we now have a sense of how that wave of immigration would turn out. If the next hundred years is at all like the last hundred—or the last five hundred—we can predict that year after year of massive immigration from the world's poorest countries into the I-7, the world's most innovative nations, would eventually tend to have effects like these:

The quality of government would fall; corruption would rise.

Social conflict would increase—and so would the risk of civil war.

Trust—and probably trustworthiness—toward strangers would decline.

Support would rise for higher minimum wages and laws making it harder to fire workers.

Innovation would decline overall, and since new innovations eventually spread across the entire planet, the entire planet would eventually lose out.

The final result of this kind of decades-long immigration wave: average incomes in the I-7 would be lower than if that massive wave of immigration had never happened, and there would be a world of slower, more sluggish growth in new science, new technology.

Of course, the descendants of immigrants would themselves certainly be better off than if their ancestors had been banned from immigrating—there's no doubt about that, for perhaps a century or maybe even longer. But over the decades—and very likely before a century had passed—the lower government quality, lower trust, and greater social conflict in the I-7 would tend to hurt the productivity, the incomes, the rates of innovation, and the long-term well-being of the descendants of those who had lived in the I-7 before the immigration wave. And crucially, humans living everywhere on the planet would lose out as the I-7 became less innovative. National economies are a team effort—especially in democracies. And some mixture of

falling national SAT scores—especially Tech History scores,

rising ethnic and cultural diversity—often spurring a racist backlash from the people whose ancestors had long lived in the I-7, and

imported cultural attitudes, including those toward issues like trust, thrift, and family ties,

would be very likely to wound the goose that lays the golden eggs of global innovation and worldwide prosperity.

Of course, these predictions are acts of imagination since they require thinking about two hypothetical scenarios. But all thinking about the effects of government policy choices are acts of imagination. Why, then, should you pay attention to these imaginary conclusions?

Because my most important claim—that culture persists and, to a substantial degree, survives the process of migration—is backed up by the types of evidence that have a lot in common with good experiments. Since 1500 people have moved around the world, and they've tended to carry much, often most, of their economic heritage with them from their old countries. Here, the countries of the Americas and Southeast Asia without large waves of high-SAT immigration are the control group, and the countries that did have big waves of high-SAT immigration—the neo-Europes and neo-Chinas, for example—are the treatment group.

And looking at shorter time horizons, the second-, third-, and even fourth-generation descendants of immigrants around the world today hold political and social attitudes a lot like those in the countries their ancestors came from long, long ago. Here the average Italian or average German is in the control group, and the Italian Americans or the German Americans are the treatment group, treated with an American culture that never fully took. One might imagine that someday, someone will invent a pill or a TikTok video or a PowerPoint slide deck that eliminates the persistence of culture. But unless that happens, you should keep on believing that, on average, migrants make the places they move to a lot like the places they left.

As we saw in the discussion of the Chinese diaspora, cultural transplant theory can, in principle, be part of a focused pro-immigration policy: if a country wants prosperity and peace over the next century, it's prudent to choose an immigration policy that raises its Tech History score; that imports cultural attitudes that are friendly to competent governance, markets, and individualism; and that gives some attention—but nowhere close to overwhelming attention—to the risks that often accompany greater cultural and ethnic diversity.

Those risks of cultural diversity, while not overwhelming, are still too big to ignore. As former President Obama recently said about the nation he led: "America is the first real experiment in building a large, multiethnic, multicultural democracy. And we don't know yet if that can hold. There haven't been enough of them around for long enough to say for certain that it's going to work."[2]

But while certainty isn't on the menu—it rarely is in the world of policy—we can still draw upon the evidence as it exists. At least in the universities if not in the newspapers, that evidence should be candidly, openly discussed. And other nations choosing their future immigration policies should place great weight on that existing evidence.

But while diversity has its risks, excellence has its rewards. Stepping outside the formal confines of the studies we've been reviewing, it should be obvious that every nation, including those in the I-7, should welcome and give instantaneous citizenship to Nobel laureates, great writers, innovative scientists from every country, full stop. I don't have a theorem or an equation to prove that. I just have the fact that one-in-a-thousand minds are rare treasures, and those human treasures should be appreciated by the leaders and the citizens of every nation. We should always welcome and always learn from the best among us.

A Fictional Ending to a True Story

At the end of Taika Waititi's excellent *Thor: Ragnarok*, we behold the complete destruction of the homeland of Thor's people, the planet Asgard, at the hands of the fire demon Surtur. Many of the people of Asgard were able to escape with the God of Thunder and so became refugees in search of a new home. They eventually found that new home: Earth—in fact, a small town on Earth, Norway's charming Tønsberg.

To lose a homeland is a great sorrow, and the movie's characters grieve that loss. But Idris Elba's character, Heimdall—an all-seeing god himself—soon brings some measure of comfort when he states, concisely, the power of the culture transplant. With these words, Heimdall reminds Thor that the culture of Asgard can and will be transplanted to their new homeland: "Asgard's not a place; it's a people."

ACKNOWLEDGMENTS

THIS IS THE FINAL BOOK IN my Singapore Trilogy. The trilogy began with *Hive Mind*, where the first country mentioned is Singapore, a nation that unsurprisingly combines high test scores, high average incomes, and high-quality governance. The second book, *10% Less Democracy*, has an entire chapter on the lessons the world's rich democracies can learn from Singapore, a nation with perhaps 50 percent less democracy than the U.S. And of course, Singapore—largely a nation of immigrants whose ancestors left southern China—illustrates cultural transplant theory.

This trilogy would not exist without the support of my longtime friends and indispensable editors, Karen Johnson and Matt DeVries. It also would not exist without the strong support of my colleagues in George Mason University's Department of Economics—who voted a decade ago to grant me the precious gift of tenure—and at GMU's Center for Study of Public Choice. The Public Choice Center has been generous in financially supporting the work that led to all three of these books. And I'm exceptionally grateful to George Mason University itself, which not only pays me a regular salary with exceptional benefits in good times and bad but which also generously funded the sabbatical that enabled me to write *The Culture Transplant*. My editor at Stanford University Press, Steve Catalano, has been a great supporter of my work and exceptional to work with—take your book proposals to him. My copyeditor Barbara Armentrout offered exceptional line edits and improved the text in ways small and large; my thanks to her. Cindy Lim and Gigi Mark of Stanford University Press made sure the editing and production process for this book all proceeded smoothly. And literary agent Margo Beth Fleming of Brockman has been indispensable as a sounding board and advisor on all three books in this trilogy.

Much of *The Culture Transplant* was written during the COVID lockdown of early 2020, in the midst of my sabbatical. During that time, Elizabeth King set aside a room in her home just so I'd have a place to write and think and work. I'm exceptionally grateful to her for that time. Earlier in the sabbatical, while I'd been on what I'd hoped would become a much longer road tour of top economics departments, I'd had excellent conversations with Aldo Rustichini of the University of Minnesota and David Cesarini of New York University that were particularly invigorating, reminders of how excellent the life of the mind can be.

I dedicate this book to the memory of my beloved father and my first real intellectual companion, Richard Olin Jones, who died too young and who deserved to live long enough to meet all of his grandchildren. A union pipefitter, exceptionally skilled at his tradecraft and respected by his coworkers, he was a model of intense focus and hard, intelligent work. I would have loved to argue about this book with him.

Your Nation's SAT Score

THE SAT SCORES ARE SIMPLE AVERAGES of the migration-adjusted State History (S), Agricultural History (A), and Technological History (T) scores discussed in chapters 2 and 3, reweighted so that every value is between 0 and 1.

SAT* scores are an optimal weighting of the S, A, and T, based on an ordinary least-squares regression of log 2002 income per person on the same migration-adjusted S, A, and T scores. Again, these are reweighted to so that every value is between 0 and 1. The regression gives overwhelming weight to Tech History, a small negative weight to Agricultural History, and almost no weight to State History.

The message of SAT* is that if you're trying to predict a nation's prosperity with just an index of S, A, and T, then you want to give almost all the weight to the T—to the Comin, Easterly, and Gong migration-adjusted year 1500 Tech History Index. To the extent that S and A are useful in predicting modern prosperity, it's mostly because they're foreshadowing T, a measure that captures later experience with technology.

Country	SAT	SAT*	Income per person, 2002
Algeria	0.56	0.80	5,769
Angola	0.16	0.15	2,232
Argentina	0.74	0.81	11,086
Australia	0.72	0.92	28,335
Austria	0.78	0.87	29,339
Bangladesh	0.54	0.56	1,696
Belarus	0.54	0.85	5,542
Belgium	0.71	0.90	27,576
Benin	0.20	0.11	1,074
Bolivia	0.50	0.33	2,497
Botswana	0.13	0.11	9,017
Brazil	0.65	0.74	7,776
Burkina Faso	0.33	0.50	1,110
Cameroon	0.27	0.12	2,037
Canada	0.73	0.86	29,865
Central African Republic	0.31	0.19	1,175
Chad	0.26	0.37	999
Chile	0.60	0.65	9,805
China	0.90	0.78	4,552
China, Hong Kong SAR	0.89	0.77	26,565
Colombia	0.51	0.59	6,382
Congo	0.22	0.16	979
Costa Rica	0.64	0.89	8,842
Croatia	0.69	0.76	10,232
Denmark	0.72	0.90	30,907
Ecuador	0.45	0.41	3,537
Egypt	0.70	0.68	3,814
El Salvador	0.51	0.57	4,935
Estonia	0.49	0.85	12,379
Ethiopia	0.61	0.52	739
Finland	0.42	0.70	26,580
France	0.81	0.87	27,123
Gabon	0.18	0.09	6,403
Germany	0.81	0.82	27,175
Ghana	0.34	0.33	2,126
Greece	0.77	0.84	18,767

Country	SAT	SAT*	Income per person, 2002
Guatemala	0.44	0.38	4,085
Guinea	0.28	0.23	2,084
Guyana	0.52	0.45	4,264
Honduras	0.50	0.54	2,604
Hungary	0.72	0.83	13,921
India	0.75	0.63	2,674
Indonesia	0.52	0.66	3,178
Iran	0.85	0.66	6,525
Ireland	0.59	0.79	36,751
Italy	0.78	0.82	26,460
Japan	0.70	0.85	26,808
Kenya	0.21	0.17	1,020
Lao People's DR	0.66	0.71	1,678
Latvia	0.51	0.85	9,275
Lesotho	0.09	0.12	2,443
Lithuania	0.54	0.88	10,349
Madagascar	0.24	0.32	745
Malaysia	0.65	0.71	9,160
Mali	0.39	0.49	977
Mauritania	0.27	0.07	1,575
Mexico	0.50	0.40	9,005
Mongolia	0.46	0.33	1,624
Morocco	0.52	0.43	3,811
Nepal	0.56	0.17	1,383
Netherlands	0.72	0.88	29,038
New Zealand	0.63	0.88	21,788
Nicaragua	0.50	0.53	3,211
Niger	0.39	0.43	806
Nigeria	0.39	0.46	947
Norway	0.63	0.91	37,148
Pakistan	0.79	0.59	2,018
Panama	0.50	0.52	6,293
Papua New Guinea	0.14	0.00	2,376
Paraguay	0.51	0.44	4,606
Peru	0.51	0.38	5,011
Philippines	0.40	0.52	4,172

Country	SAT	SAT*	Income per person, 2002
Poland	0.66	0.82	10,707
Portugal	0.79	0.95	18,154
Republic of Korea	0.72	0.88	17,225
Republic of Moldova	0.61	0.73	1,477
Romania	0.62	0.59	6,733
Russian Federation	0.56	0.79	8,309
Senegal	0.33	0.29	1,592
Sierra Leone	0.15	0.08	516
Singapore	0.83	0.75	24,013
Slovakia	0.61	0.77	12,940
South Africa	0.25	0.28	10,136
Spain	0.80	0.96	21,599
Sudan	0.49	0.30	1,806
Sweden	0.65	0.89	26,019
Switzerland	0.72	0.82	30,361
Syrian Arab Republic	0.76	0.50	3,528
Thailand	0.69	0.73	7,007
Tunisia	0.63	0.79	6,765
Turkey	0.87	0.70	6,389
Uganda	0.25	0.18	1,403
Ukraine	0.59	0.80	4,906
United Kingdom	0.75	1.00	26,134
United States	0.64	0.73	35,924
Uruguay	0.75	0.84	7,769
Uzbekistan	0.60	0.37	1,667
Venezuela	0.54	0.55	5,387
Vietnam	0.68	0.76	2,304
Zambia	0.16	0.16	839

Sources: Putterman and Weil (2010); Comin, Easterly, and Gong (2010); author's calculations.

NOTES

Introduction

1. Adam Smith, *An Inquiry into the Nature and Causes of the Wealth of Nations* (London: Printed for W. Strahan and T. Cadell in the Strand, 1776), https://archive.org/details/inquiryintonatur01smit_0.

2. Xavier Sala-i-Martin, "I Just Ran Two Million Regressions." *American Economic Review* 87, no. 2 (May 1997): 178–83.

Chapter 1: The Assimilation Myth

1. Alberto Alesina and Paola Giuliano, "Culture and Institutions," *Journal of Economic Literature* 53, no. 4 (2015): 904.

2. Jan Luiten van Zanden and Jutta Bolt, "The Maddison Project," University of Groningen (2013).

3. Edwin Williamson, *The Penguin History of Latin America,* new ed. (London: Penguin, 2003), ch. 13.

4. Alicia Vidaurreta, "Spanish Immigration to Argentina, 1870–1930," *Jahrbuch für Geschichte Lateinamerikas* 19, no. 1 (1982): 310.

5. David Rock, *Argentina, 1516–1982: From Spanish Colonization to the Falklands War* (Berkeley: University of California Press, 1985): 186.

6. Vidaurreta, "Spanish Immigration to Argentina," 310.

7. William R. Svec, "Reviewed Work: *Immigration and Nationalism: Argentina and Chile, 1890–1914* by Carl Solberg," *Hispanic American Historical Review* 50, no. 3 (August 1970): 616.

8. S. Fanny Simon, "Anarchism and Anarcho-Syndicalism in South America," *Hispanic American Historical Review* 26, no. 1 (1946): 38.

9. Juan F. Marsal, "Review: *Immigration and Nationalism: Argentina*

and Chile, 1890–1914 by Carl Solberg," *Annals of the American Academy of Political and Social Science* 392, How Wars End (November 1970): 209.

10. Bryan Caplan, "Why Should We Restrict Immigration?" *Cato Journal* 32 (2012): 13.

11. The World Values Survey website is at https://www.worldvalues survey.org/wvs.jsp.

12. The General Social Survey website is at https://gss.norc.org/.

13. Yann Algan and Pierre Cahuc, "Inherited Trust and Growth," *American Economic Review* 100, no. 5 (2010): 2060–92.

14. "Mother Who Left Baby Outside New York Restaurant in 1997 Says Arrest Was Unjust," *Associated Press*, November 26, 2017.

15. Algan and Cahuc, "Inherited Trust and Growth."

16. Daouda Sylla, "Impact of Culture on the Second Generation Immigrants' Level of Trust in Canada," PhD diss., University of Ottawa, 2014. I'm reporting the results with only regional controls, since the other kitchen-sink regressions that control for migrant education, parental education, and so on have a ton of overcontrol bias.

17. Julie Moschion and Domenico Tabasso, "Trust of Second Generation Immigrants: Intergenerational Transmission or Cultural Assimilation?" *IZA Journal of Migration* 3. no. 10 (2014): 1–30.

18. Martin Ljunge, "Trust Issues: Evidence on the Intergenerational Trust Transmission among Children of Immigrants," *Journal of Economic Behavior & Organization* 106 (2014): 175–96.

19. Order of the Sons of Italy, "A Profile of Today's Italian Americans: A Report Based on the Year 2000 Census," http://www.osia.org/wp -content/uploads/2017/05/IA_Profile.pdf.

20. Tracie McMillan, "How Italian Cuisine Became as American as Apple Pie," *National Geographic: The Plate*, May 4, 2016.

21. Garett Jones, *Hive Mind: How Your Nation's IQ Matters So Much More Than Your Own* (Stanford, CA: Stanford University Press, 2015).

22. Joan Costa-Font, Paola Giuliano, and Berkay Ozcan, "The Cultural Origin of Saving Behavior," *PLOS ONE* 13, no. 9 (2018).

23. Nicola Fuchs-Schündeln, Paolo Masella, and Hannah Paule-Paludkiewicz, "Cultural Determinants of Household Saving Behavior," *Journal of Money, Credit and Banking* 52, no. 5 (2020): 1035.

24. Alberto Alesina, Yann Algan, Pierre Cahuc, and Paola Giuliano, "Family Values and the Regulation of Labor," *Journal of the European Economic Association* 13, no. 4 (2015): 599–630.

25. Alesina et al., "Family Values and the Regulation of Labor," 617–18.

26. Alesina et al., 618.

27. Alesina et al., 618.

28. Mireia Borrell-Porta, Joan Costa-Font, and Azusa Sato, "Changing Culture to Change Society?" in *Social Economics: Current and Emerging Avenues*, ed. Joan Costa-Font and Mario Macis (Cambridge, MA: MIT Press, 2017): 261.

Chapter 2: Prosperity Migrates

1. Louis Putterman and David Weil, "Post-1500 Population Flows and the Long-Run Determinants of Economic Growth and Inequality," *Quarterly Journal of Economics* 125, no. 4 (2010): 1629.

2. Bertrand Russell, "Voice of the Sages," Appendix VII, in *The Collected Papers of Bertrand Russell*, ed. Andrew Bone, vol. 29, *Détente or Destruction, 1955–57* (London: Routledge, 2005): 365.

3. Kozo Yamamura, "The Growth of Commerce in Medieval Japan," in *The Cambridge History of Japan*, vol. 3, ed. Kozo Yamamura (Cambridge: Cambridge University Press, 1990): ch. 8, 378.

4. Colin McEvedy and Richard M. Jones, *Atlas of World Population History* Harmondsworth, UK; New York: Penguin Books, 1978); and James B. Ang, "Institutions and the Long-Run Impact of Early Development," *Journal of Development Economics* 105 (2013): 1–18.

5. Putterman and Weil, "Post-1500 Population Flows."

6. Putterman and Weil, 1628. Italics in original.

7. Putterman and Weil, 1678.

8. Putterman and Weil, 1641.

9. Throughout this book, I use standard Pearson correlations (usually denoted R or r) between two variables as a measure of percent explained of one variable by the other variable. So if I say a State History or Agricultural History measure predicts "about half" of income differences, I mean that the Pearson correlation—the most common measure of correlation—is around 0.5. Most college textbooks would instead use the *square* of these numbers as the preferred measure of percent predicted—and the square of 0.5 is of course 0.25, or 25%, but I disagree with that usage.

Why do I treat Pearson correlation as a measure of "percent predicted" or, quite informally, "percent explained"? In brief, because R is the square root of a squared percentage explained, and for practical purposes, the square root of a squared distance is the distance. You can try it out yourself in a spreadsheet—you'll find that when a correlation between two statistics is 0.3, then you'll find that knowing the values of one of the statistics helps you predict about 30% of the differences in the other. A 0.3 correlation is no small relationship, and we'll see plenty of correlations in this book bigger than that.

10. M. R. Yilmaz and Sangit Chatterjee, "Salaries, Performance, and Owners' Goals in Major League Baseball: A View through Data," *Journal of Managerial Issues* (2003): 243–55. See also Michael Friendly, "Corrgrams: Exploratory Displays for Correlation Matrices," *American Statistician* 56, no. 4 (2002): 316–24.

11. Thomas J. Sargent, "The Observational Equivalence of Natural and Unnatural Rate Theories of Macroeconomics," *Journal of Political Economy* 84, no. 3 (1976): 631–40.

Chapter 3: Places or Peoples?

1. Diego Comin, William Easterly, and Erick Gong, "Was the Wealth of Nations Determined in 1000 BC?" *American Economic Journal: Macroeconomics* 2, no. 3 (2010): 71

2. Zahra Ahmad, "Why Modern Mortar Crumbles but Roman Concrete Lasts Millennia," *Science*, July 3, 2017, https://www.science.org/content/article/why-modern-mortar-crumbles-roman-concrete-lasts-millennia.

3. Peter N. Peregrine and Melvin Ember, eds., *Encyclopedia of Prehistory* (New York: Springer Science & Business Media, 2001): xix.

4. Jane Jacobs, *The Economy of Cities* (New York: Vintage, 2016).

5. Comin, Easterly, and Gong, "Was the Wealth of Nations," 84.

6. Catherine Rampell, "Was Today's Poverty Determined in 1000 B.C.?," *Economix* (blog), *New York Times*, August 2, 2010, https://economix.blogs.nytimes.com/2010/08/02/was-todays-poverty-determined-in-1000-b-c.

7. Comin, Easterly, and Gong, "Was the Wealth of Nations," 84.

8. Tongue in cheek, of course. I'm just using ordinary least squares (OLS) regression.

9. Enrico Spolaore and Romain Wacziarg, "How Deep Are the Roots of Economic Development?," *Journal of Economic Literature* 51, no. 2 (2013): 325–69.

10. Christian Biémont and Cristina Vieira, "Junk DNA as an Evolutionary Force," *Nature* 443, no. 7111 (2006): 521–24; Alexander F. Palazzo and T. Ryan Gregory, "The Case for Junk DNA," *PLOS GENETICS* 10, no. 5 (2014), https://doi.org/10.1371/journal.pgen.1004351; W. Ford Doolittle, "Is Junk DNA Bunk? A Critique of ENCODE," *Proceedings of the National Academy of Sciences* 110, no. 14 (2013): 5294–300.

11. Enrico Spolaore and Romain Wacziarg, "The Diffusion of Development," *Quarterly Journal of Economics* 124, no. 2 (2009): 469–529.

12. Quamrul Ashraf and Oded Galor, "The 'Out of Africa' Hypothesis, Human Genetic Diversity, and Comparative Economic Development," *American Economic Review* 103, no. 1 (2013): 1–46; Quamrul H. Ashraf and Oded Galor, "The Macrogenoeconomics of Comparative Development," *Journal of Economic Literature* 56, no. 3 (2018): 1119–55.

13. Adam Smith, *An Inquiry into the Nature and Causes of the Wealth of Nations* (London: Printed for W. Strahan and T. Cadell in the Strand, 1776), https://archive.org/details/inquiryintonatur01smit_0.

14. Franck Prugnolle, Andrea Manica, François Balloux, "Geography predicts neutral genetic diversity of human populations," *Current Biology* 15, no. 5 (2005): R159–60.

15. For many of these measures, see Areendam Chanda, C. Justin Cook, and Louis Putterman, "Persistence of Fortune: Accounting for Population Movements, There Was No Post-Columbian Reversal," *American Economic Journal: Macroeconomics* 6, no. 3 (2014): 1–28.

16. Morgan Kelly, "The Standard Errors of Persistence," unpublished manuscript, posted June 14, 2019, https://ssrn.com/abstract=3398303.

17. Morgan Kelly's critique, known generally as the problem of "spatial autocorrelation," applies to any cross-country comparison, not just those associated with the Deep Roots literature. For example, countries that are pro-market and prosperous tend to be near each other; countries with higher levels of gender equality and high education tend to be near each other. Entire schools of thought are built around claims that these correlations are robust and real and represent some kind of causation, but these correlations almost never take account of the fact that "near = similar" and that there are only one or two dozen unique countries, with the rest being near-clones of those one or two dozen. All of this was well summarized in Waldo Tobler's First Law of Geography: "Everything is related to everything else, but near things are more related than distant things." Waldo R. Tobler, "A Computer Movie Simulating Urban

Growth in the Detroit Region," *Economic Geography* 46, Supplement: Proceedings (1970): 236.

Chapter 4: The Migration of Good Government

1. Lecture in 1755, quoted in Dugald Stewart, "Account of the Life and Writings of Adam Smith LL.D.," in *The Collected Works of Dugald Stewart*, vol. 10 (Edinburgh: Thomas Constable and Company, 1793, section IV, 25.

2. Louis Putterman and David Weil, "Post-1500 Population Flows and the Long-Run Determinants of Economic Growth and Inequality," *Quarterly Journal of Economics* 125, no. 4 (2010): 1652.

3. Edward L. Glaeser, Rafael La Porta, Florencio Lopez-de-Silanes, and Andrei Shleifer, "Do Institutions Cause Growth?" *Journal of Economic Growth* 9, no. 3 (2004): 271–303.

4. Putterman and Weil, 1653.

5. John Adams, *Novanglus,* no. 7. March 6, 1775. Internet Archive, 84. https://archive.org/details/novanglusmassach00adams/page/78/mode/2up. Emphasis in original.

6. Gregory Clark, *A Farewell to Alms* (Princeton, NJ: Princeton University Press, 2008).

7. Glaeser et al., "Do Institutions Cause Growth?," 276.

8. Daniel Kaufmann, Aart Kraay, and Pablo Zoido-Lobatón, *Governance Matters II: Updated Indicators for 2000–01*, vol. 2772 (Washington, DC: World Bank Publications, 2002): 5.

9. James B. Ang, "Institutions and the Long-Run Impact of Early Development," *Journal of Development Economics* 105 (2013): 1–18.

10. The World Governance Indicators (WGI) are regularly updated, and the project is funded by the World Bank. It is available online at http://info.worldbank.org/governance/wgi/.

11. Garett Jones, *10% Less Democracy: Why You Should Trust Elites a Little More and the Masses a Little Less* (Stanford, CA: Stanford University Press, 2020).

12. Key exception: the northern region of Chile was part of the southern portion of the relatively prosperous Inca empire.

13. Daron Acemoglu, Simon Johnson, and James A. Robinson, "Reversal of Fortune: Geography and Institutions in the Making of the Modern World Income Distribution," *Quarterly Journal of Economics* 117, no. 4 (2002): 1279.

14. Areendam Chanda, C. Justin Cook, and Louis Putterman, "Per-

NOTES TO CHAPTER 5   173

sistence of Fortune: Accounting for Population Movements, There Was No Post-Columbian Reversal," *American Economic Journal: Macroeconomics* 6, no. 3 (2014): 1–28.

Chapter 5: Our Diversity Is Our ____

1. Jonas Hjort, "Ethnic Divisions and Production in Firms," *Quarterly Journal of Economics* 129, no. 4 (2014): 1899.

2. Gloria Mwaniga, "How a Kenyan Flower Producer Bloomed through COVID-19," *IFC Insights*, September 2020, https://www.ifc.org/wps/wcm/connect/news_ext_content/ifc_external_corporate_site/news+and+events/news/insights/i15-kenya-flowers.

3. Hjort, "Ethnic Divisions and Production," 1929.

4. Hjort, 1929.

5. Hjort, 1902–3.

6. Michael Rothschild, and Joseph E. Stiglitz, "Increasing Risk: I. A Definition," *Journal of Economic Theory* 2, no. 3 (1970): 225–43; George J. Stigler, "The Economics of Information," *Journal of Political Economy* 69, no. 3 (1961): 213–25; Thomas J. Sargent, *Dynamic Macroeconomic Theory* (Cambridge, MA: Harvard University Press, 2009).

7. Robert Shimer, "The Diamond-Mortensen-Pissarides Contribution to Economics," unpublished manuscript, University of Chicago, October 20, 2010. http://sites.tufts.edu/yioannides/files/2012/09/Shimer-Pissarides.pdf.

8. Tracy Kidder, *The Soul of a New Machine* (Boston: Little, Brown, 1981).

9. Katherine Y. Williams and Charles A. O'Reilly III, "Demography and Diversity in Organizations: A Review of 40 Years of Research," *Research in Organizational Behavior* 8 (1998): 70–140.

10. Williams and O'Reilly, "Demography and Diversity," 120.

11. Williams and O'Reilly, 121.

12. Williams and O'Reilly, 121.

13. Williams and O'Reilly, 121.

14. Williams and O'Reilly, 120.

15. Williams and O'Reilly, 80.

16. Susan E. Jackson, Aparna Joshi, and Niclas L. Erhardt, "Recent Research on Team and Organizational Diversity: SWOT Analysis and Implications," *Journal of Management* 29, no. 6 (2003): 810. Italics in original

17. Daan Van Knippenberg and Michaela C. Schippers, "Work Group Diversity," *Annual Review of Psychology* 58 (2007): 518.

18. Elizabeth Mannix and Margaret A. Neale, "What Differences Make a Difference? The Promise and Reality of Diverse Teams in Organizations," *Psychological Science in the Public Interest* 6, no. 2 (2005): 31.

19. Mannix and Neale, "What Differences Make a Difference?," 35.

20. Karsten Jonsen, Susan C. Schneider, and Martha L. Maznevski, "Diversity—A Strategic Issue?" In *Diversity in the Workplace*, ed. Stefan Gröschl (London and New York: Routledge, 2016): 29.

21. Jonsen, Schneider, and Maznevski, "Diversity—A Strategic Issue?," 35.

22. Hans Van Dijk, Marloes L. Van Engen, and Daan Van Knippenberg, "Defying Conventional Wisdom: A Meta-Analytical Examination of the Differences between Demographic and Job-Related Diversity Relationships with Performance," *Organizational Behavior and Human Decision Processes* 119, no. 1 (2012): 38.

23. Ashli B. Carter, and Katherine W. Phillips, "The Double-Edged Sword of Diversity: Toward a Dual Pathway Model," *Social and Personality Psychology Compass* 11, no. 5 (2017): e12313; Payton A. Small, Brenda Major, and Cheryl Kaiser, "Making Diversity Work for Everybody? The Double-Edged Sword of All-Inclusive Diversity," *Personality and Social Psychology Bulletin*, October 2021, https://doi.org/10.1177%2F01461672211047016; Nai-Wen Chi, Yin-Mei Huang, and Shu-Chi Lin, "A Double-Edged Sword? Exploring the Curvilinear Relationship Between Organizational Tenure Diversity and Team Innovation: The Moderating Role of Team-Oriented HR Practices," *Group & Organization Management* 34, no. 6 (2009): 698–726.

24. Daniel B. Klein and Charlotta Stern, "Professors and Their Politics: The Policy Views of Social Scientists," *Critical Review* 17, no. 3–4 (2005): 257–303; Neil Gross and Ethan Fosse, "Why Are Professors Liberal?," *Theory and Society* 41, no. 2 (2012): 127–68; Noah Carl, "Can Intelligence Explain the Overrepresentation of Liberals and Leftists in American Academia?," *Intelligence* 53 (2015): 181–93.

25. Robin J. Ely and David A. Thomas, "Getting Serious about Diversity," *Harvard Business Review* 98, no. 6 (2020): 114–22. The authors argue that their new-and-improved case for diversity will be stronger and more practical than the older cases, and maybe a decade from now we'll know if they were right. But for now, the lesson is that at the current state of knowledge, the current business case for diversity as a boost to business performance is muddled at best.

26. Vivian Hunt, Lareina Yee, Sundiatu Dixon-Fyle, and Sara Prince,

Delivering through Diversity, Report, McKinsey & Company, January 2018, https://www.mckinsey.com/business-functions/people-and-organ izational-performance/our-insights/delivering-through-diversity.

27. Jean Tirole, *The Theory of Corporate Finance* (Princeton, NJ: Princeton University Press, 2010).

28. Robert D. Putnam, *Bowling Alone: The Collapse and Revival of American Community* (New York: Simon and Schuster, 2000).

29. Robert D. Putnam, "E Pluribus Unum: Diversity and Community in the Twenty-First Century," *Scandinavian Political Studies* 30, no. 2 (2007): 137–74.

30. Peter Thisted Dinesen, Merlin Schaeffer, and Kim Mannemar Sønderskov, "Ethnic Diversity and Social Trust: A Narrative and Meta-Analytical Review." *Annual Review of Political Science* 23 (2020): 441–65.

31. Joan Esteban and Debraj Ray, "On the Salience of Ethnic Conflict," *American Economic Review* 98, no. 5 (2008): 2185.

32. Klaus Desmet, Ignacio Ortuño-Ortín, and Romain Wacziarg, "Culture, Ethnicity, and Diversity," *American Economic Review* 107, no. 9 (2017): 2479.

33. Desmet, Ortuño-Ortín, and Wacziarg, "Culture, Ethnicity, and Diversity," 2481.

34. James Habyarimana, Macartan Humphreys, Daniel N. Posner, and Jeremy M. Weinstein, "Why Does Ethnic Diversity Undermine Public Goods Provision?," *American Political Science Review* 101, no. 4 (2007): 709.

35. Holger Stichnoth and Karine Van der Straeten, "Ethnic Diversity, Public Spending, and Individual Support for the Welfare State: A Review of the Empirical Literature." *Journal of Economic Surveys* 27, no. 2 (2013): 368.

Chapter 6: The I-7

1. Wolfgang Keller, "International Technology Diffusion." *Journal of Economic Literature* 42, no. 3 (2004): 752.

2. An obvious exception: if the idea is "ability to destroy the world," that's an idea that should go undiscovered if at all possible. Other damaging ideas would fall in the same bad-to-discover category.

3. OECD, "OECD Triadic Patents," in *OECD Factbook 2013: Economic, Environmental and Social Statistics* (OECD Publishing 2018): 6. https://doi.org/10.1787/factbook-2013-en.

4. OECD, "OECD Triadic Patents."

5. Nature Index, https://www.natureindex.com/annual-tables/2018/country/all.

6. Edinaldo Tebaldi and Bruce Elmslie, "Does Institutional Quality Impact Innovation? Evidence from Cross-Country Patent Grant Data," *Applied Economics* 45, no. 7 (2013): 887–900.

7. Tebaldi and Elmslie, "Does Institutional Quality Impact Innovation?," 890.

8. Tebaldi and Elmslie, 890.

9. Reminder: This is my way of saying the Pearson correlation is about 0.7.

10. Cong Wang, "Can Institutions Explain Cross Country Differences in Innovative Activity?" *Journal of Macroeconomics* 37 (2013): 128–45.

11. Wang, "Can Institutions Explain Cross Country Differences," 143.

12. Jonathan Eaton and Samuel Kortum, "International Technology Diffusion: Theory and Measurement," *International Economic Review* 40, no. 3 (1999): 537.

13. Edwin Mansfield and Anthony Romeo, "Technology Transfer to Overseas Subsidiaries by U.S.-Based Firms," *Quarterly Journal of Economics* 95 (1980): 737–50.

14. Mansfield and Romeo, "Technology Transfer to Overseas Subsidiaries," 738, note 3.

15. Mansfield and Romeo, 738.

16. Mansfield and Romeo, 746.

17. Mansfield and Romeo, 746, note 19.

18. Mansfield and Romeo, 742.

19. Tracy Kidder, *The Soul of a New Machine* (Boston: Little, Brown, 1981).

20. Michele Boldrin and David K. Levine, *Against Intellectual Monopoly* (Cambridge: Cambridge University Press, 2008).

21. Bronwyn H. Hall, Jacques Mairesse, and Pierre Mohnen, "Measuring the Returns to R&D," in *Handbook of the Economics of Innovation*, ed. Bronwyn H. Hall and Nathan Rosenberg, vol. 2, 1069.

22. Hall, Mairesse, and Mohnen, "Measuring the Returns to R&D," 1072.

23. Hall, Mairesse, and Mohnen, 1072.

Chapter 7: The Chinese Diaspora: Building the Capitalist Road

1. Jan Priebe and Robert Rudolf, "Does the Chinese Diaspora Speed Up Growth in Host Countries?" *World Development* 76 (2015): 250.

2. Amy Chua, *World on Fire: How Exporting Free Market Democracy Breeds Ethnic Hatred and Global Instability* (New York: Anchor, 2004).

3. Lynn Pan, *Sons of the Yellow Emperor: The Story of the Overseas Chinese* (London: Secker & Warburg, 1990): 132.

4. James E. Rauch and Vitor Trindade, "Ethnic Chinese Networks in International Trade," *Review of Economics and Statistics* (2002): 116–30; their data draws in large part from Dudley L. Poston Jr., Michael Xinxiang Mao, and Mei-Yu Yu, "The Global Distribution of the Overseas Chinese around 1990," *Population and Development Review* (1994): 631–45.

5. Milton E. Osborne, *Southeast Asia: An Introductory History* (Sydney: Allen & Unwin, 2016): 117.

6. Paul J. Bolt, *China and Southeast Asia's Ethnic Chinese: State and Diaspora in Contemporary Asia* (Westport, CT: Praeger, 2000), 24–25.

7. Henry Wai-chung Yeung, "The Dynamics of Southeast Asian Chinese Business," *Handbook of Research on Asian Business*, ch. 18 (Cheltenham, UK: Elgar, 2007): 356.

8. Steven Ratuva, "Ethnicity, Reform and Affirmative Action in Malaysia," in *Politics of Preferential Development: Trans-Global Study of Affirmative Action and Ethnic Conflict in Fiji, Malaysia and South Africa* (Canberra: ANU Press, 2013): 202.

9. Ratuva, "Ethnicity, Reform and Affirmative Action," 202–3.

10. U.S. Department of State, *2018 Investment Climate Statements: Malaysia*, n.d., https://www.state.gov/reports/2018-investment-climate-statements/malaysia/.

11. Pan, *Sons of the Yellow Emperor*, 133.

12. Priebe and Rudolf, "Does the Chinese Diaspora Speed Up Growth," 249.

13. Priebe and Rudolf, 249.

14. Priebe and Rudolf, 249.

15. Priebe and Rudolf, 250.

16. James D. Gwartney, Robert A. Lawson, Joshua C. Hall, and Ryan H. Murphy, *Economic Freedom of the World* (Washington, DC: Cato Institute; Vancouver, BC: Fraser Institute, 2018).

17. "Chinese Are Thriving in Laos, but the Community Is Resented," *New York Times*, August 14, 1964, 3.

18. Howard W. French, *China's Second Continent: How a Million Migrants Are Building a New Empire in Africa* (New York: Vintage, 2014).

Chapter 8: The Deep Roots across the Fifty United States

1. Scott L. Fulford, Ivan Petkov, and Fabio Schiantarelli, "Does It Matter Where You Came From? Ancestry Composition and Economic Performance of U.S. Counties, 1850–2010," *Journal of Economic Growth* 25, no. 3 (2020): 341.

2. U.S. Department of Homeland Security, *Fiscal Year 2019 Entry/Exit Overstay Report* (Washington, D.C.: DHS, March 30, 2020), https://www.dhs.gov/sites/default/files/publications/20_0513_fy19-entry-and-exit-overstay-report.pdf.

3. U.S. Department of Homeland Security, "Profiles of Naturalized Citizens, 2017," database, last updated September 12, 2019, https://www.dhs.gov/profiles-naturalized-citizens-2017-countryhttps://www.dhs.gov/profiles-naturalized-citizens-2017-country.

4. Fulford, Petkov, and Schiantarelli, "Does It Matter Where You Came From?," 344.

5. Francesco Giavazzi, Ivan Petkov, and Fabio Schiantarelli, "Culture: Persistence and Evolution," *Journal of Economic Growth* 24, no. 2 (2019): 117–54.

6. Bryan Caplan, "Why Should We Restrict Immigration?" *Cato Journal* 32 (2012): 14.

7. Giavazzi, Petkov, and Schiantarelli, "Culture," 119.

8. Alex Nowrasteh and Andrew Forrester, *Trust Doesn't Explain Regional US Economic Development and Five Other Theoretical and Empirical Problems with the Trust Literature*, working paper no. 57, Cato Institute, January 6, 2020, https://www.cato.org/publications/working-paper/trust-doesnt-explain-regional-us-economic-development-five-other#.

9. Ryan H. Murphy and Alex Nowrasteh, "The Deep Roots of Economic Development in the US States: An Application of Putterman and Weil (2010)," *Journal of Bioeconomics* 20, no. 2 (2018): 227–42.

Je ne sais quoi

1. Jared Diamond, "Reversals of National Fortune, and Social Science Methodologies," *Proceedings of the National Academy of Sciences* 111, no. 50 (2014): 17713.

2. Edward Stone, "An Account of the Success of the Bark of the Willow Tree in the Cure of Agues," *Philosophical Transactions* 53 (1763).

3. Philippa Martyr, "Hippocrates and Willow Bark: What You Know about the History of Aspirin Is Probably Wrong," *The Conversation*, October 18, 2020, https://theconversation.com/hippocrates-and-willow -bark-what-you-know-about-the-history-of-aspirin-is-probably-wrong -148087.

4. Tyler Cowen, "Be Suspicious of Simple Stories," TEDxMidAtlantic, November 2009, https://www.ted.com/talks/tyler_cowen_be_suspicious _of_simple_stories?language=en.

Conclusion: The Goose and the Golden Eggs

1. "The Goose and the Golden Egg," *The Æsop for Children* (New York: Rand McNally, 1919), presented by Library of Congress, https:// read.gov/aesop/091.html.

2. Quoted in Jeffrey Goldberg, "Why Obama Fears for Our Democracy," *The Atlantic*, November 16, 2020.

BIBLIOGRAPHY

Abascal, Maria, and Delia Baldassarri. "Love Thy Neighbor? Ethnoracial Diversity and Trust Reexamined." *American Journal of Sociology* 121, no. 3 (2015): 722–82.

Acemoglu, Daron, Simon Johnson, and James A. Robinson. "Reversal of Fortune: Geography and Institutions in the Making of the Modern World Income Distribution." *Quarterly Journal of Economics* 117, no. 4 (2002): 1231–94.

Adams, John. *Novanglus,* no. 7. March 6, 1775. Internet Archive, 78–94. https://archive.org/details/novanglusmassach00adams/page/78/mode/2up.

Ahmad, Zahra. "Why Modern Mortar Crumbles but Roman Concrete Lasts Millenia." *Science,* July 3, 2017. https://www.science.org/content/article/why-modern-mortar-crumbles-roman-concrete-lasts-millennia.

Alesina, Alberto, Yann Algan, Pierre Cahuc, and Paola Giuliano. "Family Values and the Regulation of Labor." *Journal of the European Economic Association* 13, no. 4 (2015): 599–630.

Alesina, Alberto, and Paola Giuliano. "Culture and Institutions." *Journal of Economic Literature* 53, no. 4 (2015): 898–944.

Algan, Yann, and Pierre Cahuc. "Inherited Trust and Growth." *American Economic Review* 100, no. 5 (2010): 2060–92.

Ang, James B. "Institutions and the Long-Run Impact of Early Development." *Journal of Development Economics* 105 (2013): 1–18.

Ashraf, Quamrul H., and Oded Galor. "The Macrogenoeconomics of

Comparative Development." *Journal of Economic Literature* 56, no. 3 (2018): 1119–55.

———. "The 'Out of Africa' Hypothesis, Human Genetic Diversity, and Comparative Economic Development." *American Economic Review* 103, no. 1 (2013): 1–46.

Biémont, Christian, and Cristina Vieira. "Junk DNA as an Evolutionary Force." *Nature* 443, no. 7111 (2006): 521–24.

Boldrin, Michele and David K. Levine. *Against Intellectual Monopoly.* Cambridge: Cambridge University Press, 2008.

Bolt, Paul J. *China and Southeast Asia's Ethnic Chinese: State and Diaspora in Contemporary Asia.* Westport, CT: Praeger, 2000.

Borrell-Porta, Mireia, Joan Costa-Font, and Azusa Sato. "Changing Culture to Change Society?" In *Social Economics: Current and Emerging Avenues,* edited by Joan Costa-Font and Mario Macis. Cambridge, MA: MIT Press, 2017.

Caplan, Bryan. "Why Should We Restrict Immigration?" *Cato Journal* 32 (2012): 5–24.

Carl, Noah. "Can Intelligence Explain the Overrepresentation of Liberals and Leftists in American Academia?" *Intelligence* 53 (2015): 181–93.

Carter, Ashli B., and Katherine W. Phillips. "The Double-Edged Sword of Diversity: Toward a Dual Pathway Model." *Social and Personality Psychology Compass* 11, no. 5 (2017): e12313.

Chanda, Areendam, C. Justin Cook, and Louis Putterman. "Persistence of Fortune: Accounting for Population Movements, There was No Post-Columbian Reversal." *American Economic Journal: Macroeconomics* 6, no. 3 (2014): 1–28.

Chi, Nai-Wen, Yin-Mei Huang, and Shu-Chi Lin. "A Double-Edged Sword? Exploring the Curvilinear Relationship between Organizational Tenure Diversity and Team Innovation: The Moderating Role of Team-Oriented HR Practices." *Group & Organization Management* 34, no. 6 (2009): 698–726.

Chua, Amy. *World on Fire: How Exporting Free Market Democracy Breeds Ethnic Hatred and Global Instability.* New York: Anchor, 2004.

Clark, Gregory. *A Farewell to Alms.* Princeton, NY: Princeton University Press, 2008.

Comin, Diego, William Easterly, and Erick Gong. "Was the Wealth of Nations Determined in 1000 BC?" *American Economic Journal: Macroeconomics* 2, no. 3 (2010): 65–97.

Costa-Font, Joan, Paola Giuliano, and Berkay Ozcan. "The Cultural

Origin of Saving Behavior." *PLOS ONE* 13, no. 9 (2018). https://doi.org/10.1371/journal.pone.0202290.

Desmet, Klaus, Ignacio Ortuño-Ortín, and Romain Wacziarg. "Culture, Ethnicity, and Diversity." *American Economic Review* 107, no. 9 (2017): 2479–513.

Diamond, Jared. "Reversals of National Fortune, and Social Science Methodologies." *Proceedings of the National Academy of Sciences* 111, no. 50 (2014): 17709–14.

Dinesen, Peter Thisted, Merlin Schaeffer, and Kim Mannemar Sønderskov. "Ethnic Diversity and Social Trust: A Narrative and Meta-Analytical Review." *Annual Review of Political Science* 23 (2020): 441–65.

Doolittle, W. Ford. "Is Junk DNA Bunk? A Critique of ENCODE." *Proceedings of the National Academy of Sciences* 110, no. 14 (2013): 5294–300.

Eaton, Jonathan, and Samuel Kortum. "International Technology Diffusion: Theory and Measurement." *International Economic Review* 40, no. 3 (1999): 537–70.

Ely, Robin J., and David A. Thomas. "Getting Serious about Diversity." *Harvard Business Review* 98, no. 6 (2020): 114–22.

Esteban, Joan, and Debraj Ray. "On the Salience of Ethnic Conflict." *American Economic Review* 98, no. 5 (2008): 2185–202.

French, Howard W. *China's Second Continent: How a Million Migrants Are Building a New Empire in Africa.* New York: Vintage, 2014.

Friendly, Michael. "Corrgrams: Exploratory Displays for Correlation Matrices." *American Statistician* 56, no. 4 (2002): 316–24.

Fuchs-Schündeln, Nicola, Paolo Masella, and Hannah Paule-Paludkiewicz. "Cultural Determinants of Household Saving Behavior." *Journal of Money, Credit and Banking* 52, no. 5 (2020): 1035–70.

Fulford, Scott L., Ivan Petkov, and Fabio Schiantarelli. "Does It Matter Where You Came From? Ancestry Composition and Economic Performance of U.S. Counties, 1850–2010." *Journal of Economic Growth* 25, no. 3 (2020): 341–80.

Glaeser, Edward L., Rafael La Porta, Florencio Lopez-de-Silanes, and Andrei Shleifer. "Do Institutions Cause Growth? " *Journal of Economic Growth* 9, no. 3 (2004): 271–303.

Giavazzi, Francesco, Ivan Petkov, and Fabio Schiantarelli. "Culture: Persistence and Evolution." *Journal of Economic Growth* 24, no. 2 (2019): 117–54.

Goldberg, Jeffrey. "Why Obama Fears for Our Democracy." *Atlantic*, 16 November 2020.

Gross, Neil, and Ethan Fosse. "Why Are Professors Liberal?" *Theory and Society* 41, no. 2 (2012): 127–68.

Gwartney, James D., Robert A. Lawson, Joshua C. Hall, and Ryan H. Murphy, with Pál Czeglédi, Rosemarie Fike, Fred McMahon, and Carlos Newland. *Economic Freedom of the World: 2018 Annual Report.* Washington, DC: Cato Institute; Vancouver, BC: Fraser Institute, 2018.

Habyarimana, James, Macartan Humphreys, Daniel N. Posner, and Jeremy M. Weinstein. "Why Does Ethnic Diversity Undermine Public Goods Provision?" *American Political Science Review* 101, no. 4 (2007): 709–25.

Hall, Bronwyn H., Jacques Mairesse, and Pierre Mohnen. "Measuring the Returns to R&D." In *Handbook of the Economics of Innovation,* edited by Bronwyn H. Hall and Nathan Rosenberg, vol. 2, 1033–82. Amsterdam: Elsevier, 2010.

Heston, Alan, Robert Summers, and Bettina Aten. "Penn World Table Version 6.2." Center for International Comparisons of Production, Income and Prices at the University of Pennsylvania, 2006. https://datacentre.chass.utoronto.ca/pwt62/.

Hjort, Jonas. "Ethnic Divisions and Production in Firms." *Quarterly Journal of Economics* 129, no. 4 (2014): 1899–946.

Hunt, Vivian, Lareina Yee, Sundiatu Dixon-Fyle, and Sara Prince. *Delivering through Diversity.* Report. McKinsey & Company, January 2018. https://www.mckinsey.com/business-functions/people-and-organizational-performance/our-insights/delivering-through-diversity.

Jackson, Susan E., Aparna Joshi, and Niclas L. Erhardt. "Recent Research on Team and Organizational Diversity: SWOT Analysis and Implications." *Journal of Management* 29, no. 6 (2003): 801–30.

Jacobs, Jane. *The Economy of Cities.* New York: Vintage, 2016.

Jones, Garett. *Hive Mind: How Your Nation's IQ Matters So Much More Than Your Own.* Stanford, CA: Stanford University Press, 2015.

———. *10% Less Democracy: Why You Should Trust Elites a Little More and the Masses a Little Less.* Stanford, CA: Stanford University Press, 2020.

Jonsen, Karsten, Susan C. Schneider, and Martha L. Maznevski. "Diversity—A Strategic Issue?" In *Diversity in the Workplace,* ed. Stefan Gröschl (London and New York: Routledge, 2016): 29-62.

Kaufmann, Daniel, and Aart Kraay. *Worldwide Governance Indicators.* Washington, DC: World Bank, 2021.

Kaufmann, Daniel, Aart Kraay, and Pablo Zoido-Lobatón. *Governance*

Matters II: Updated Indicators for 2000–01. Vol. 2772. Washington, DC: World Bank Publications, 2002.

Kelly, Morgan. "The Standard Errors of Persistence." Unpublished manuscript, posted June 14, 2019. https://ssrn.com/abstract=3398303.

Kidder, Tracy. *The Soul of a New Machine.* Boston: Little, Brown, 1981.

Klein, Daniel B., and Charlotta Stern. "Professors and Their Politics: The Policy Views of Social Scientists." *Critical Review* 17, no. 3–4 (2005): 257–303.

Langguth, Jack. "Chinese Are Thriving in Laos, but the Community Is Resented." *New York Times,* August 14, 1964. https://nyti.ms/3HReFqU.

Ljunge, Martin. "Trust Issues: Evidence on the Intergenerational Trust Transmission among Children of Immigrants." *Journal of Economic Behavior & Organization* 106 (2014): 175–96.

Mansfield, Edwin, and Anthony Romeo. "Technology Transfer to Overseas Subsidiaries by U.S.-Based Firms." *Quarterly Journal of Economics* 95, no. 4 (1980): 737–50.

Marsal, Juan F. "Review of Carl Solberg, *Immigration and Nationalism: Argentina and Chile, 1890–1914.*" *Annals of the American Academy of Political and Social Science* 392, no. 1 (1970): 209–10.

Martyr, Philippa. "Hippocrates and Willow Bark: What You Know about the History of Aspirin Is Probably Wrong." *Conversation,* October 18, 2020. https://theconversation.com/hippocrates-and-willow-bark-what-you-know-about-the-history-of-aspirin-is-probably-wrong-148087.

McEvedy, Colin, and Richard Jones. *Atlas of World Population History.* Harmondsworth, UK; New York: Penguin Books, 1978.

McMillan, Tracie. "How Italian Cuisine Became as American as Apple Pie." The Plate. *National Geographic,* May 4, 2016. https://www.nationalgeographic.com/culture/article/how-italian-cuisine-became-as-american-as-apple-pie.

Mwaniga, Gloria. "How a Kenyan Flower Producer Bloomed through COVID-19." *IFC Insights,* September 2020. https://www.ifc.org/wps/wcm/connect/news_ext_content/ifc_external_corporate_site/news+and+events/news/insights/i15-kenya-flowers.

Moschion, Julie, and Domenico Tabasso. "Trust of Second-Generation Immigrants: Intergenerational Transmission or Cultural Assimilation?" *IZA Journal of Migration* 3, no. 10 (2014): 1–30.

Murphy, Ryan H., and Alex Nowrasteh. "The Deep Roots of Economic Development in the US States: An Application of Putterman and Weil (2010)." *Journal of Bioeconomics* 20, no. 2 (2018): 227–42.

Nature Index. "2018 Tables: Countries/territories." Based on data from January 1, 2017, to December 31, 2017. https://www.natureindex.com /annual-tables/2018/country/all.

Nowrasteh, Alex, and Andrew Forrester. *Trust Doesn't Explain Regional U.S. Economic Development and Five Other Theoretical and Empirical Problems with the Trust Literature.* Working paper no. 57. Cato Institute. January 6, 2020. https://www.cato.org/publications/working -paper/trust-doesnt-explain-regional-us-economic-development-five -other#.

OECD (2018). *OECD Factbook 2013: Economic, Environmental and Social Statistics.* Paris: OECD Publishing, 2013. https://doi.org/10.1787/ factbook-2013-en.

Order of the Sons of Italy. "A Profile of Today's Italian Americans: A Report Based on the Year 2000 Census." 2003. http://www.osia.org /wp-content/uploads/2017/05/IA_Profile.pdf.

Osborne, Milton E. *Southeast Asia: An Introductory History.* 12th ed. Sydney: Allen & Unwin, 2016.

Palazzo, Alexander F., and T. Ryan Gregory. "The Case for Junk DNA." *PLOS GENETICS* 10, no. 5 (2014). https://doi.org/10.1371/journal .pgen.1004351.

Pan, Lynn. *Sons of the Yellow Emperor: The Story of the Overseas Chinese.* London: Secker & Warburg, 1990.

Poston, Dudley L., Jr., Michael Xinxiang Mao, and Mei-Yu Yu. "The Global Distribution of the Overseas Chinese around 1990." *Population and Development Review* (1994): 631–45.

Priebe, Jan, and Robert Rudolf. "Does the Chinese Diaspora Speed Up Growth in Host Countries?" *World Development* 76 (2015): 249–62.

Prugnolle, Franck, Andrea Manica, and François Balloux. "Geography Predicts Neutral Genetic Diversity of Human Populations." *Current Biology* 15, no. 5 (2005): R159–160.

Putterman, Louis, and David N. Weil. "Post-1500 Population Flows and the Long-Run Determinants of Economic Growth and Inequality." *Quarterly Journal of Economics* 125, no. 4 (2010): 1627–82.

Putnam, Robert D. *Bowling Alone: The Collapse and Revival of American Community.* New York: Simon and Schuster, 2000.

———. "E Pluribus Unum: Diversity and Community in the Twenty-First Century. The 2006 Johan Skytte Prize Lecture." *Scandinavian Political Studies* 30, no. 2 (2007): 137–74.

Rampell, Catherine. "Economix: Was Today's Poverty Determined in 1000 B.C.?" *New York Times*, August 2, 2010. https://economix.blogs .nytimes.com/2010/08/02/was-todays-poverty-determined-in-1000 -b-c.

Ratuva, Steven. "Ethnicity, Reform and Affirmative Action in Malaysia." In *Politics of Preferential Development: Trans-Global Study of Affirmative Action and Ethnic Conflict in Fiji, Malaysia and South Africa*, 195–218. Canberra: ANU Press, 2013.

Rauch, James E., and Vitor Trindade. "Ethnic Chinese Networks in International Trade." *Review of Economics and Statistics* 84, no. 1 (2002): 116–30.

Rock, David. *Argentina, 1516–1982: From Spanish Colonization to the Falklands War.* Berkeley: University of California Press, 1985.

Russell, Bertrand. "Voice of the Sages," Appendix VII. In *The Collected Papers of Bertrand Russell.* Vol. 29, *Détente or Destruction, 1955–57*, edited by Andrew Bone, 363–65. London: Routledge, 2005.

Sala-i-Martin, Xavier. "I Just Ran Four Million Regressions." *American Economic Review* 87, no. 2 (May 1997): 178–83.

Rothschild, Michael, and Joseph E. Stiglitz. "Increasing Risk: I. A Definition." *Journal of Economic Theory* 2, no. 3 (1970): 225–43.

Sargent, Thomas J. *Dynamic Macroeconomic Theory.* Cambridge, MA: Harvard University Press, 2009.

———. "The Observational Equivalence of Natural and Unnatural Rate Theories of Macroeconomics." *Journal of Political Economy* 84, no. 3 (1976): 631–40.

Shimer, Robert. "The Diamond-Mortensen-Pissarides Contribution to Economics." Unpublished manuscript. October 20, 2010. http://sites .tufts.edu/yioannides/files/2012/09/Shimer-Pissarides.pdf.

Simon, S. Fanny. "Anarchism and Anarcho-Syndicalism in South America." *Hispanic American Historical Review* 26, no. 1 (1946): 38–59. https://doi.org/10.2307/2507692.

Small, Payton A., Brenda Major, and Cheryl Kaiser. "Making Diversity Work for Everybody? The Double-Edged Sword of All-Inclusive Diversity." *Personality and Social Psychology Bulletin*, October 2021. https://doi.org/10.1177%2F01461672211047016.

Smith, Adam. *An Inquiry into the Nature and Causes of the Wealth of Nations*. London: Printed for W. Strahan and T. Cadell in the Strand, 1776. https://archive.org/details/inquiryintonatur01smit_0.

Stewart, Dugald. "Account of the Life and Writings of Adam Smith LL.D." In *The Collected Works of Dugald Stewart*, vol. 10, 1–98. Edinburgh: Thomas Constable and Company, 1793. https://socialsciences.mcmaster.ca/econ/ugcm/3ll3/smith/dugald.

Stichnoth, Holger, and Karine Van der Straeten. "Ethnic Diversity, Public Spending, and Individual Support for the Welfare State: A Review of the Empirical Literature." *Journal of Economic Surveys* 27, no. 2 (2013): 364–89.

Spolaore, Enrico, and Romain Wacziarg. "The Diffusion of Development." *Quarterly Journal of Economics* 124, no. 2 (2009): 469–529.

———. "How Deep Are the Roots of Economic Development?" *Journal of Economic Literature* 51, no. 2 (2013): 325–69.

Stigler, George J. "The Economics of Information." *Journal of Political Economy* 69, no. 3 (1961): 213–25.

Stone, Edward. "An Account of the Success of the Bark of the Willow Tree in the Cure of Agues." *Philosophical Transactions of the Royal Society of London* 53, Letter XXXII (1763): 195–200. https://royalsocietypublishing.org/doi/epdf/10.1098/rstl.1763.0033.

Svec, William R. "Reviewed Work: *Immigration and Nationalism: Argentina and Chile, 1890–1914* by Carl Solberg." *Hispanic American Historical Review* 50, no. 3 (August 1970): 616.

Sylla, Daouda. "Impact of Culture on the Second Generation Immigrants' Level of Trust in Canada." PhD diss., University of Ottawa, 2014.

Tebaldi, Edinaldo, and Bruce Elmslie. "Does Institutional Quality Impact Innovation? Evidence from Cross-Country Patent Grant Data." *Applied Economics* 45, no. 7 (2013): 887–900.

Tirole, Jean. *The Theory of Corporate Finance*. Princeton, NJ: Princeton University Press, 2010.

Tobler, Waldo R. "A Computer Movie Simulating Urban Growth in the Detroit Region." *Economic Geography* 46, Supplement: Proceedings (1970): 234–40.

U.S. Department of Homeland Security. *Fiscal Year 2019 Entry/Exit Overstay Report*. Washington, DC: DHS, March 30, 2020. https://www.dhs.gov/sites/default/files/publications/20_0513_fy19-entry-and-exit-overstay-report.pdf.

———. "Profiles on Naturalized Citizens, 2017 Country." Database. Last updated September 12, 2019. https://www.dhs.gov/profiles-naturalized-citizens-2017-country.

U.S. Department of State. "2018 Investment Climate Statements: Malaysia." n.d. https://www.state.gov/reports/2018-investment-climate-statements/malaysia/.

Van Dijk, Hans, Marloes L. Van Engen, and Daan Van Knippenberg. "Defying Conventional Wisdom: A Meta-analytical Examination of the Differences between Demographic and Job-Related Diversity Relationships with Performance." *Organizational Behavior and Human Decision Processes* 119, no. 1 (2012): 38–53.

Van Knippenberg, Daan, and Michaela C. Schippers. "Work Group Diversity." *Annual Review of Psychology* 58 (2007): 518.

van Zanden, Jan Luiten, and Jutta Bolt. "The Maddison Project." University of Groningen, 2013. https://www.rug.nl/ggdc/historicaldevelopment/maddison.

Vidaurreta, Alicia. "Spanish Immigration to Argentina, 1870–1930." *Jahrbuch für Geschichte Lateinamerikas* 19, no. 1 (1982): 285–319.

Wang, Cong. "Can Institutions Explain Cross Country Differences in Innovative Activity?" *Journal of Macroeconomics* 37 (2013): 128–45.

Williams, Katherine Y., and Charles A. O'Reilly III. "Demography and Diversity in Organizations: A Review of 40 Years of Research." *Research in Organizational Behavior* 8 (1998): 70–140.

Williamson, Edwin. *The Penguin History of Latin America.* New ed. London: Penguin, 2003.

Yamamura, Kozo. "The Growth of Commerce in Medieval Japan." In *The Cambridge History of Japan*, vol. 3, edited by Kozo Yamamura. Cambridge: Cambridge University Press, 1990.

Yeung, Henry Wai-chung. "The Dynamics of Southeast Asian Chinese Business." *Handbook of Research on Asian Business*, ch. 18. Cheltenham, UK: Edward Elgar Publishing, 2007.

Yilmaz, M. R., and Sangit Chatterjee. "Salaries, Performance, and Owners' Goals in Major League Baseball: A View through Data." *Journal of Managerial Issues* 15, no. 2 (Summer 2003): 243–55. https://www.jstor.org/stable/40604428.

INDEX

abortion, 145

Acemoglu, Daron: on European colonization, 76; on Mexico's population of European descent, 30; on rich vs. poor places, 76

acetaminophen/Tylenol, 155

Adams, John: on a republic as government of laws, 69

Aesop's story of the goose who laid golden eggs, 156–57

Afghanistan: income per person, 50; institutional quality, 74; Technological History, 50, 53, 74

Africa: Chinese immigration to, 136–37; migration from, 39; technological sophistication in, 46; technology in North Africa, 46; trustingness in, 15

Africa, sub-Saharan, 4–5, 31; economic conditions, 28–29, 50–51; vs. Eurasia, 61; genetic diversity in, 61; income per person, 50–51; poverty in, 50–51, 74, 75; technology in, 46; vs. Western Europe, 50–51

African Americans, 139, 140–41, 149

age diversity, 87

Agricultural History (long experience living amid settled agriculture): migration-adjusted vs. migration-unadjusted, 34–35, 36–37; as national prosperity predictor, 45, 51–54, 62, 66, 73–74, 77, 135, 148–50, 158, 159, 163–66; Putterman and Weil on, 32, 33–35, 36, 37, 38–39, 40, 41, 48–49, 51, 52, 62, 166; relationship to government corruption, 66, 102, 149; relationship to government quality, 66, 72–73, 74, 77, 102, 107, 118, 135, 149; relationship to income per person, 52–54, 73–74, 75, 135, 163–66; relationship to personal and economic freedom, 149–50; relationship to social capital, 149; relationship to Technological History, 62–63, 163

Alesina, Alberto: on change in cultural values, 6; on social consequences of close-knit families, 22–24, 139